Kara Richardson Whitely

the weight of being

How I Satisfied My Hunger for Happiness

SEAL PRESS

Seal Press
Hachette Book Group
1700 Fourth Street
Berkeley, California
sealpress.com

Printed in the United States of America

First Edition: July 2018

Published by Seal Press, an imprint of Perseus Books, LLC, a subsidiary of Hachette Book Group, Inc. The Seal Press name and logo is a trademark of the Hachette Book Group.

The Hachette Speakers Bureau provides a wide range of authors for speaking events. To find out more, go to www.hachettespeakersbureau.com or call (866) 376-6591.

The publisher is not responsible for websites (or their content) that are not owned by the publisher.

Print book interior design by Amy Quinn

Library of Congress Cataloging-in-Publication Data has been applied for.

ISBNs: 978-1-58005-647-2 (paperback), 978-1-58005-648-9 (ebook)

LSC-C

10 9 8 7 6 5 4 3 2 1

To Chris, Anna, Emily, and Elliott—
the inspiration for all I do

Part One

The doctor's hand moved across a thick red line on a graph. She pressed firmly down and made a dot.

My daughter, then five years old, had just slid over the line into the overweight swath of the growth chart. I wanted to curl up into my flesh, all three hundred pounds of it.

"You don't want to be there," the doctor said gently to Anna. "It's just a little over, but you might want to try little things to cut back and move a little more."

I'm sorry. I'm so sorry, I thought while stroking my little girl's blonde hair, a nod to the Scandinavian roots on my side of the family. She had my gray-blue eyes. She had my skin, which was set to sunburn at the slightest sunscreen slip. She had my piano-perfect fingers, and now, it seemed, she was about to inherit my weight problem. I couldn't let that happen.

But she's not fat, I thought. *She's not like me. I can't let her be like me.* My weight was all consuming; it was the thing I most wanted to lose, yet it had stuck with me the most tenaciously for the past three decades, regardless of how many times I signed up for diet programs, bought new exercise equipment (my latest, a rowing machine, was currently collecting dust in my office), or wrote down resolutions—"give up sugar" and "exercise every day"—or goals—"lose 100 pounds this year" and "fit into a size 12 by the wedding"—in my weight loss journal.

I could mostly rationalize away all those failed efforts. After all, a raft of studies proved how tough it was to lose weight and keep it off. And I was relatively healthy (I didn't have diabetes, heart disease, or any other syndrome associated with fat people) and somewhat fit, so I could brush aside the fact that I was powerless to change my weight.

But now, my fat was encroaching on my daughter's life. I wanted to defend her against the scourge that made everything from sleeping to moving difficult. I couldn't control my eating. How would I control hers?

But I made Anna's food choices for her. I was the mother, the person saying "yes" when she asked for another helping of Goldfish crackers. I was the one caving in to her nightly requests for ice cream. I loved ice cream. We all did. But what my family didn't know was that I was dipping into the half-gallon container while they were out during the day, and then secretly replacing the empty container and starting all over again the next day.

My relationships with food and my body were twisted, torturous affairs. The kind that filled me with angst and immobility. And now I was passing this on to my daughter.

"We'll do better," I told the doctor. But as I said it, I worried the intention fell flat, like any of my weight loss pursuits, announcements, and campaigns that started with me buying a whole lot of things—from fat-free this and that to a series of exercise videos and weight loss hypnosis CDs—and would go nowhere.

I gathered my purse and walked Anna out the door. We stopped at the reception desk only to collect a sticker for her bravery. I tried to smile but felt sick inside, knowing that Anna's problem started with me.

"Mommy, can we get a treat here?" she asked, as we walked past a neighboring pharmacy.

"Not today, sweetie," I said, as we reached the elevator.

"But Moooooooooom," she cried, drawing disapproving stares from passersby.

I knew all about those stares. I had been bullied about my weight since I was nine years old. People made fun of my protruding belly, my expanding rear. It made me a big target, the butt of jokes.

I put those thoughts out of my mind. Anna wasn't me. I smiled at my daughter, who was still looking at me beseechingly. "Okay, but something healthy," I conceded. I grabbed a Rice Krispies bar from my bag, hoping it said fat-free somewhere on the label.

Later that evening at dinner with my fit, marathoner husband, we talked about how we wanted to stay healthy as a family.

"Oh, boy," Chris said, almost in a joking manner, the same way he did if he discovered all the cookies were missing. It was a comment he made as if he'd heard it before.

Anna looked down at her rice and chicken. I didn't want her to be self-conscious. We never sat down at the table to discuss my weight, so why would we be doing that for her?

I tried to quickly diffuse the conversation. "Well, how about we start saving sweets for the weekends? How about we sign Anna up for swim classes?"

"Okay," Anna said.

We left it at that.

A few nights later, I helped Anna on with her pajamas. "I'm fat," she declared.

"Honey, you're not fat. I'm fat," I blurted without thinking.

"I knew that. I just didn't want to hurt your feelings," Anna said, looking away as if she was afraid she was going to get in trouble for speaking the truth.

At school, she and her fellow kindergarteners had been trying on the word *fat* for size, seeing how their classmates reacted to the epithet. A few kids, even one heavier than Anna, already dubbed Anna fat, she had confessed. I was enraged, told the teacher, and had the girl apologize to my daughter. I worried they were calling her that because of how I looked.

"It's about being healthy," I said, gulping away a tear. I had been an overweight kid, a too-big-to-miss target for bullies since the age of nine, when my parents divorced and I hid in the pantry, binging to drown out their screaming. When I was twelve, I put on forty pounds over the summer after my brother's almost-adult friend sexually assaulted me. Fat was my protection but also my curse. The more life hurt, the more I ate and, of course, the more I gained. The more I gained, the worse I felt.

I had to keep Anna from ever feeling the way I did. I needed to do something this very moment to show my daughter a healthy way of living. She should not have to experience the weight of simply being. *My* weight of being. It buried me.

If she was going to feel good about herself, change had to start with me.

◇◇◇

I was forty-one and weighed three hundred pounds. I had weighed less. I had weighed more. But this was where my body seemed to want to be. Three hundred pounds. Or maybe this was where *I* wanted to be? Either way, my weight defined me and had defined me for years, decades filled with agony and a healthy serving of self-loathing.

Anna's doctor would have said I was morbidly obese. I had the kind of fat that bulged over the waistline of my jeans and into my lap. The kind of fat that made plastic lawn chairs—and other kinds of seats—beg for mercy when I tried to squeeze into them. The kind of fat that forced people to notice my girth before they noticed me.

I knew I was more than a number, more than my weight. Yet being fat was a part of who I was, part of how people knew me. For years, I believed that I didn't want to be fat and tried to swat down pounds with every diet and fitness regimen imaginable. I even went so far as to train for and hike Mount Kilimanjaro, Africa's highest peak—three times.

Once, after a 120-pound weight loss to a low of 240 pounds on my six-foot frame, I climbed Kilimanjaro to prove I was invincible.

Less than a year later, I gained more than half of the weight back while pregnant with Anna. Desperate to feel in control of my weight, I returned to the mountain. I was out of shape, ill-equipped, and in absolute denial about my food issues—so much so that I binged the night before the seven-day trek. Spoiler alert: I didn't make it to the top that time.

On my third and last trek up the mountain, I weighed three hundred pounds, yet made it to the summit—at more than nineteen thousand feet—succeeding against the bets of the snickering porters. I hiked as much as fifteen hours a day to conquer the more than fifty-mile push up the mountain, and I didn't drop more than a dozen pounds. I returned home just as I had left: fat.

Though my body seemed to like being three hundred pounds, I was never happy with this state. Therefore, I was never happy, carrying around that extra flesh, flesh that sat on my belly, hips, and thighs, that sagged from my arms like bat wings.

I was not just fat but big. Six feet tall. Like my mother's, my weight tended to settle on my lower half. If I met someone while sitting down, they often couldn't tell how heavy I was. I didn't want them to see that, when I stood, I needed to push on something, the table in front of me, the window ledge next to me, the seat of the chair below me, to give me enough leverage to land on my feet without tipping. Then all was revealed. The weight that I carried down below was stuffed into size twenty-eight pants that really should have been size thirty-two, but most stores didn't carry that size. I was always pushing plus-size limits.

Naked, my scars were visible. Remnants of an accident from when I was eighteen months old and boiling water from a flip-top kettle spilled over me. They start just below my neck and extend down between my collarbones and breasts, making plunging necklines a problem. *Sexy* and *voluptuous* were not possibilities anyhow because I was flat on top, with no extra flesh to help me there.

What were less visible were the scars I carried inside. Depression had also weighed me down since I was a kid. As much as I tried to shut it out, I was never able to ignore the voice that overshadowed everything I did. *Don't work out—you should be working instead.* The voice, my longest-standing frenemy, said everything I did was a complete sham. That I was a failure before I even started the day. The voice, I suspect, kept me at that weight, even though I desperately didn't want to be there.

And yet, there I stayed. Simply put, I was ginormous.

With the marching orders from Anna's doctor and a five-year-old daughter who was just about normal weight—for now—I needed to defy that voice, defy what my body seemed to want—and do something drastic.

When I was pregnant with Anna, my first child, I was transformed from someone who had hiked to the Roof of Africa to a person who could barely walk across the living room floor. Sciatica, a nerve condition, sent lightning bolts down my leg with every step. When I tried to heal my body with yoga, dropping into a wide-angle sitting bend, my belly touched the floor in an embarrassing lump, and I inevitably injured myself and regretted an overzealous practice that put me further out of commission, again. The ice and snow came the last four months of my pregnancy, so even though I loved to walk, I was afraid to put one foot in front of the other outdoors.

All the while, I wondered what kind of parent I would be. I'd always had a complex relationship with my parents, especially my father, who essentially abandoned us after his divorce from my mother. When he did show up, he caused trouble and seemed annoyed his kids were around.

I joked my child would be better off raised by wolves than by me. The prospect of being responsible for another life was daunting, intimidating in a way that no one talked about. If I couldn't take care of myself—and by that I meant my weight—how could I take care of a child?

Meanwhile, I gave myself permission to eat for two, slurping milkshakes (calcium!) and devouring cheeseburgers (protein!) all the way to a seventy-pound-plus pregnancy gain.

Despite all this, Anna came out perfect, at seven pounds eleven ounces.

I landed at three hundred pounds.

When I was pregnant with my second daughter, Emily, I gained only fifteen pounds, all of it lost with the birth, and landed at three hundred pounds, again. That time, not having put on any additional weight, it was a victory.

My husband didn't gain an ounce. And he never did.

I'm married to a marathoner, a man who runs hours at a time just to get a run in. The father of my two girls is perfect when it comes to weight. Food in. Food out. He has ice cream and BBQ ribs when he wants to. He exercises when he wants to. That is his life.

When he took two hours for a run, I got maybe fifteen minutes to walk around the block while he showered. I complained about the imbalance but rarely did anything to rectify it or demand my own time to exercise.

These habits, the ones that kept me immobile and roiled in anxiety, that kept me eating to stuff down anxiety and depression, were filtering down to my daughter.

Sure, I could have put us on a family diet. But I found that the more I dieted, the further I got from real food. I made smoothies with protein powders and artificial sweeteners and chemicals to make up for carbs and fats and real nutrients. I felt very processed. And incredibly hungry after restricting myself. I didn't want to trigger that never-ending cycle for Anna—dieting and binging and binging and dieting—only to end up with one result: more weight gain.

While the girls were little, my weight and my life overwhelmed me. I'd buy processed food and uninspired produce at Target when I ran out to buy diapers for Emily just to get dinner on the table. For all my obsession with food, cooking was a chore. Sure, watching the Food Channel while on the elliptical inspired me, but my culinary ambitions shrank when I powered through the grocery aisles while keeping Anna from grabbing everything she wanted and Emily from wailing loud enough to be heard in the women's shoes aisle.

With two kids, I lived on autopilot, trying to manage a full-time job as a marketing coordinator and part-time gig as an author and motivational speaker, a family, and a life while sleep deprived. I survived on empty calories—clearing off the girls' plates, thrusting my hand into the cereal box—and generally whatever food was in front of me. Stuffing my face made it easy to forget that all I wanted was to make it to the girls' ever receding bedtime, when I could finally lie down and get some rest, at least until one of them woke up again.

Chris's bedtime routine involved chasing the kids around the house. Or, rather, holding the baby and singing "Attack Baby" while Anna squealed with joy.

"Come on, let's get on with it. Bedtime. Stories. Sleep," I'd said.

"You don't have to be so aggravated at everything," Chris would say.

"But I do."

I often thought that if I had more money, more something, I'd be happier, thinner. I could buy better food, I would grill the most tender organic meats. I would get more help, maybe even hire a personal chef. I needed help. Mountains of laundry rose on my bed each day, ready for folding, only to be swept to the floor when the next load arrived until I was forced to send my kids off to school in wrinkled garments.

Every spilled sippy cup was a pain in my outsized ass, and, hurried and hassled, I made sure my thin husband knew it by grumbling while I sopped up mess after mess. Truthfully, I caused many of the messes as I rushed through the dishes and life. I'd knock over a glass or the dish soap, and suds would seep out and drip to the floor.

If only I could clean up my own mess. Stress was eating me alive, and I in turn was eating everything. Not so much binging as saturating myself with food to cope with the constant noise in my mind. I never actually felt hunger because I used every opportunity to eat, compulsively, gobbling my way through the day: muffins with the girls' breakfast. A doughnut in the rare quiet moments after they left for school and day care. A cereal bar on the train into the office. A fully loaded coffee and an orange-glazed scone when I got to work—just to tide me over until lunch. Chipotle steak salad and chips at the afternoon meal. Munchkins with my three o'clock coffee. Roasted nuts on the train home. Another cereal bar for a snack. Roasted chicken for dinner. Ice cream for dessert.

Yet chicken nuggets was all I could manage to prepare for my family for dinner. I was suffering food exhaustion, too disgusted and bloated to be civil to my sweet husband, too frazzled and overwhelmed to provide a healthy example to my impressionable children. My rage boiled over like an unattended pot of Kraft Mac & Cheese noodles.

My husband wanted to make some changes, too. He wanted to move from our creaky condo with the grumpy neighbor to a house with a yard where our children could play. But we couldn't afford to move. We were stuck. A binger in every sense of the word, I had troubled financial habits—as poor as my eating habits. My past was marred by frantic payday loans that enabled me to spend beyond my means.

When we got married, I didn't think ahead to what life would be like with children. I didn't know Chris, and I needed to talk about roles—who would do what. Instead, we just fell into doing certain things. I never pushed for those conversations, maybe because whenever I looked at Chris, his James Dean good looks, his career ambition that led him to the executive track at work, his athleticism, I worried that I didn't deserve him. How could he be *mine*? We had been friends who grew into something more.

Know this about Chris: he sees the world differently. Maybe that's what allowed him to love me. And maybe because he loved me—he's the one who gets my jokes—I did an outsized portion of the child care and work around the house to feel worthy of him. I'd absorb a kid's snow day, a sick day, a last-minute diaper blowout for that. I knew my husband loved and appreciated me, but I couldn't help wondering whether my weight somehow served him.

One evening when Chris unloaded the dishwasher and left the clean Tupperware on the counter, the only counter in our kitchen available for chopping, plating, stirring, mail sorting, and more, my head felt like it would explode. Did he leave it for me to put away because he had the upper

hand in our relationship? Did he think he could just dump
the grunt work on me?

"If you're leaving that for me to do, I have other shit to
do," I snapped, and threw open the cabinet door so hard it
nearly smacked me in the head on the rebound.

My hands and mind tried to match and stack Tupperware like a fast-paced puzzle never to be completed.
Nothing would fit. The containers that I used for leftovers,
leftovers I often ate myself, teetered, guaranteeing disaster
for the next person who tried to pull one out—usually me.

Just like the grocery store, the kitchen also gave me
amnesia. I forgot why I was there and what I needed to do,
even if it was something simple like stepping in for a pair
of scissors. I'd spot the Nutella below the windowsill, and
instead of grabbing the shears, I'd open the next drawer
down for a spoon, unscrew the lid, and scoop away at the
hazelnut.

My kids enjoyed Nutella on toast.

I enjoyed it straight up.

Nutella was my *yes* food. If I saw something—a latte,
pancakes, crepes—made with Nutella, I automatically
wanted it. Having it in the house was dangerous. But after
Anna tried it on graham crackers and fell in love with it, I
didn't want to deny her access.

Other times, while loading the dishwasher, I'd notice
the Rice Krispies bars jutting out of the cabinet. I'd grab

myself one, maybe two, sometimes three, crinkling the wrappers and putting them in the garbage, forgetting all about the dirty dishes. In that moment, I ruined all that I was striving for. All I might have gained from my rare workout that morning.

It was almost as if any task that required me to be in the kitchen came with a requisite consumption of at least five hundred calories. And I found myself in the kitchen a lot.

I liked to blame food, or my husband, for my problems, but maybe *I* was the problem. Was I on the verge of losing my kids, my husband, my everything, all because of my weight?

Six weeks after Emily was born, I started to work again. My fingers got back into the rhythm of the workday. One afternoon, as I went for my afternoon caffeine reboot, I noticed the coffee ring stain on my desk had been reestablished. It was nice to have a cup and be productive in peace.

That was until Emily's day care called and said she had developed a troubling cough and needed to be picked up right away. I grabbed the stroller and walked out the door, crossed the street, and all at once I heard a click, a whooshing sound, then a boom. It was as if space and time had stopped.

Was it a nail gun? But I didn't see construction nearby.

Or maybe an air-powered wrench removing lug nuts? But I was well away from Andre's auto mechanic shop.

And then, a sharp pain stabbed my back, as if someone was poking me with a dagger. But no one was there.

"What the . . . *Ow!*" I screamed. I swiveled around, my back pulsating. I was afraid to put my hand on the spot where the pain was coming from, but I had to press down, to somehow make it stop hurting.

Could a bee have stung me?

I reached below my poly-blend blue shirt, the one with a nice Greek Isle perfectly-cloudless-day feel to it, and touched where my shirt met my too-taut waistband. At once, my fingers were wet. It wasn't sweat. It was blood.

That sound. I knew what it was. It was a gun. The long echo. The click. The boom. I'd been shot.

Summit, New Jersey, is a town where Mercedes-Benz and Volvos alternate in the school drop-off lines; a place where landscapers descend in a swarm to tend postage-stamp-sized lawns, blowing every stray leaf out of sight; a place where towering oaks surround stone-fortified estates owned by Wall Street wizards.

There weren't shootings in Summit. But I'd been shot, and as I reached for my phone, my hands were shaking so badly it took me three times to type in 911. Across the street, I saw kids running around the corner.

"911, what's your emergency?"

"This sounds crazy, but I think I was just shot," I said. "It might have been a BB gun."

"Madam, where are you?"

I was standing at the corner of Walnut Street and

Beauvoir, one hand resting on Emily's empty stroller, not even a block from my house.

"I could be wrong, but this is so weird. My back is bleeding and it really hurts. I heard a bang."

As I said the words, I wondered whether sleep deprivation had caught up with me. Would I be the laughingstock of the town: not just the fat lady, but the fat, crazy lady who imagined she was shot? An obese Chicken Little.

Just as I started to doubt myself, three cop cars pulled up, surrounding me. A detective approached and then, with my permission, examined the hole in my back.

Officers canvassed the block looking for a culprit. One detective stayed with me and the ambulance pulled up. By the time I had finished telling the detective what happened, a female officer appeared across the street holding a sawed-off pellet gun in one hand and gripping the arm of a seventeen-year-old named Dan with the other.

Two other teens joined him at the curbside, where they were instructed to sit and wait. Heads down, they looked at the ground, not me. I still couldn't believe that I had been shot. That someone would do this to me. Someone would use my backside for target practice. But it was true and it was awful.

I yelled across the street, "What the fuck were you thinking? You weren't. You're damn lucky my daughter wasn't in this stroller. I wouldn't be so calm as I am now, you little shits."

I felt the urge to kick all three of them where they sat, but the officer pulled me back. At that point, I didn't care that they were teenagers; I wanted at them. My heart raged inside, pounding as if I had just sprinted down the street.

A rescue squad member offered to take me to the hospital up the hill, but I knew it would be faster for me to walk there, like I did each time I was in labor. Besides, it was a mere flesh wound. The damage was more emotional than physical.

The detective told me that the boy would be charged with aggravated assault with a deadly weapon and that a colleague would be in touch for more information. And, "I just need to take a picture of the wound."

He lifted my shirt, the fabric ripping away from the wound, and took a photo of my backside. The sting of humiliation was worse than the sting of the injury.

"Are you going to be alright?" the detective asked.

"I'll be okay," I said, giving the kids one last evil eye. I tried to walk away bravely but nearly tripped on the curb in front of me. I wanted to be cool, calm, and collected, but inside I was Jell-O.

As soon as I turned away, I started to cry, a wobbling overflow of tears, and used my sleeve to wipe my eyes, which exposed the wound to the wind. I climbed the steps of my daughter's day care, punched in the security code, and worried that the boys had seen me and would know where to find my daughter. I had to walk down that street every day to get my girl. Would they bring real firepower next time? Would I be targeted again because of my size? Did they intentionally aim for my ass? Why would someone do that to me?

Because I'm fat. I believed I had brought the shooting on myself.

In my mind, I could hear what the kids must have said before they aimed and fired: "Get her right in the ass."

"You can't miss it."

As a fat person, I was used to being a target.

When I started getting heavier around age twelve, I became fodder for bullies, who prank-called my house after school and left fake love letters in my locker.

The taunting continued to that day. I never knew when a random teenager (or an adult) would call out an obnoxious comment as they drove by. *Hey, fat ass!* was popular.

Mind you, I was the one walking. Getting exercise. How was that helpful?

And then there was the one where a guy pointed me out to his friend and laughed. "Hey, there's one for you."

I wanted to tell them that I already had a man. Something I knew they wouldn't believe. Often, I don't believe it myself.

It's true that my ass is fat, but these jibes hurt my soul. They made me feel less human for being bigger than most humans.

They made me want to be skinnier, only I got fatter by binging away the pain of feeling small inside.

When I returned home with my daughter and put her down for a nap, I unwrapped a mini ice cream sandwich, placed another on stand-by (I'd picked up smaller ones for portion control), and called Chris.

"Are you okay? Oh my God," he said. "Should I come home now?"

"I'm fine. I'm fine," I assured him. He had a new job at the Weather Channel and I didn't want to bother him. Besides, it would take him at least an hour to get home.

But I wasn't okay. With Emily napping, I took a shower to wash off the shame of it all. The water stung like a punishment as it beat through the Band-Aid on my back.

When I got out, I stood dripping by the window, trying to see if the kid who shot me was on his porch. I could see it from my window. I couldn't tear my eyes away, except to dash to the kitchen for another ice cream sandwich.

◇◇◇

"Now we've both been shot."

Though we hadn't spoken in months, I had called my father, craving sympathy.

He was talking about his Vietnam service, where he served as a Navy Seal. He had been shot, stabbed, and stitched up before heading home as a different person. He had turned into someone who wouldn't sit in a restaurant with his back to the door. He didn't want us to startle him out of a nap for fear he would hurt us, a war-driven instinct. Now, having been shot was one of the few things we had in common. Somehow that knowledge left me feeling emptier. I had just wanted him to say, "Oh, sweetie. Are you okay?" but that's not what I heard.

I heard plenty of other things.

Right after the shooting, I longed for fresh air but was afraid to leave the house, worried that the teens would hunt me down again. It wasn't like I could cut my hair or slip on a pair of sunglasses and go incognito. I had a very distinctive pear shape: smallish on top, wider than most people thought possible at the hips. I couldn't hide from them, or myself.

It may have been unusual to see a big lady walking around town, but I liked to walk, liked to hike, even if my weight didn't go anywhere and it could be hazardous to my dignity. My pants were so wide they would often sag at the rear, exposing my underwear. My thighs rubbed together, wearing away the fabric of my jeans on my inner thighs and creating gaping holes.

"There's that big, fat lady again," a kid said one day.

His mother looked at me in horror, then pulled him aside to tell him that wasn't a nice way to talk about people. "But she *is* fat," I heard him say.

She took his chin in her hand and made him look her straight in the eyes.

"That's. Not. Nice," she said, making sure I heard.

A few days later, when the detective called, I didn't walk to the police station, even though it was just a few blocks away. I was nervous even stepping into the station, though I was used to being around police from my years as a newspaper reporter. To hide their shaking, I shoved my hands in my pockets, the sliver of fabric tight to my hips, trying to hold myself together until the juvenile detective pushed open a heavy door and led me back to his office. His desk was filled with photos of his own kids. I was there to tell my story and to answer a simple question: "Do you want to press charges?"

Part of me wondered whether pressing charges would only send this kid off into a spiral of disaster. As a reporter, I once interviewed a teenage graffiti artist who was caught and jailed, and he told me about all the cool new graffiti techniques he picked up in the slammer.

I didn't want to push this kid Dan on the path toward delinquency. But at the same time, I didn't want to look the other way. He'd hurt me, made me fearful in my own neighborhood, fearful in my own oversized body. Out and about in my neighborhood, I carried this fear with me, along with the pain of being shot. My wound was now surrounded by a purple and red bruise the size of a softball that highlighted the stretch marks on my otherwise alabaster back.

I wanted this boy to be punished for that very intentional act. He was seventeen, an almost-adult, and I couldn't let it go, just as I couldn't let go of my panic and dread since the shooting.

The detective showed me a photo of the wound, a puffy and red hole in my flesh. As far as crime photos went, this was a G-rated piece of evidence, but just seeing it sent me right back to the point of impact, when the pellet pierced my skin.

I pressed my pen to the paper and signed. Doing so terrified me but also made me feel powerful. Fat or not, I wasn't going to let anyone treat me this way, not in my own town, on my own street. I was taking a stand, against the bully who had shot me and against all the bullies in my life. Pressing charges, signing that paper, made me feel bigger, not in body but in spirit. Now they were going to have to fear me.

I almost killed my mother when I was born.

She and my father had moved to Canada, where he taught engineering at a university. She had my two brothers, Bryan and Derek, before she gave birth to me, each of us two years apart. My parents were moving quickly to build their family, and maybe with good reason: on their wedding day, my father suffered a severe heart attack that brought the festivities to a stop. Doctors gave him six months to live. But, a warrior Navy Seal, he defied expectations.

By the time my mother was pregnant with me, they'd been married five years, and he was working at another university in Ontario. She had given up her nursing job, struggling just to keep up with her little guys. But it wasn't just pregnancy that slowed her down. A blood clot—a deep vein thrombosis—lodged in her leg as I grew in her belly and threatened to break loose and put an end to us both.

By the time she was diagnosed, she could barely make it out of a chair. And she was told not to—the exact opposite treatment for a blood clot today, when many doctors advise patients to keep moving. They put her on blood thinners.

Homebound and terrified in the final months of the pregnancy, she wanted me out of her—safer in the outside world for both of us. A few days before I was due (I'm prompt if nothing else), she pushed me out using Lamaze breathing techniques, something relatively unheard of at the time. No painkillers, just pushing and breathing at the hospital.

A husky German nurse had warned her, "That won't work."

But it did. I came into the world by the power of breath, sweat, and profanity at eight pounds eleven ounces—the heaviest of all her babies.

Shortly after I was born, my father got a job at Queen's University, in Kingston, Ontario, and our family settled in the Thousand Islands community of Gananoque. We had a mile-long driveway that got so socked in during the winter that we had to take snowmobiles to catch the school bus.

For my father, who had returned from Vietnam with a Purple Heart, our new home was a haven, or at least his version of a haven. While the rest of us thrilled to the call of loons and played outside, he transformed the cottage down the hill into a workshop, where he amassed guns and learned to reshell bullets.

He was a survivalist intent on preparing for the long Ontario winters, when the Northern Lights would dance in the night sky. He even built a covered ramp from the woodshed to the house so that if there was a true snowfall for the ages, we wouldn't have to venture out in it for more firewood.

Summer in Ontario, short-lived as it was, was idyllic, a time of hope. My mother would drive our station wagon to the top of the hill where she worked in Mrs. Nuttall's soccer-field-sized garden in exchange for produce. With the help of that produce, we mostly lived off the grid, with no television or phone and instead communicating by two-way radio.

Life there could be lonely, so I spent a lot of time in Mrs. Nuttall's garden, too. An octogenarian who used to teach in a one-room schoolhouse, Mrs. Nuttall didn't seem to mind when I chased her chickens into the henhouse while she and my mother tied back tomatoes and trellised cucumbers.

It was a *Little House on the Prairie* kind of existence, and we all got into the swing of it, my mother, especially, who decided to start a garden of her own. I loved to twirl through the rows of beans, peas, and sunflowers that towered over my toddling legs, giggling myself into oblivion before retreating to my favorite spot—a rock formation under a canopy of trees nestled next to our house. I liked to imagine that it was a spot where fairies congregated.

When I was six years old, my grandmother Margaret— my father's mother—came to live in Gananoque for no other reason than to be near me and my brothers. She and my dad had a strained relationship; he'd always blamed Margaret for his fractured childhood, which included her marrying five times to stay afloat. I, on the other hand, was thrilled by her arrival; she was the grown-up who loved to treat me, spoiling me with chocolate instead of the carob from the health food store that my mother liked.

Margaret also arrived with several steamer trunks of fabric, thread, and sequins and proceeded to sew most of my clothing, each piece perfectly shaped around my slightly protruding belly, each making me feel special and wrapped in love. My favorite outfit was a periwinkle gingham dress. It came complete with a sun bonnet and was perfect for playing in the garden with my brothers. We'd chase each other around the raspberry, blueberry, and strawberry patches that gave us the fruit my mother made into jam to be spread on her homemade bread. The raspberries took root everywhere, but I could never have too many. I'd pop them on my fingertips, like puffy red nail polish, and then into my mouth.

My mother gathered fresh zucchini and carrots, which she grated into bread that tasted more like cake, along with

cucumbers, which she transformed into pickles in our basement through the winter, the mason jars lined up in neat
rows. She planned for our future, planting seeds that would
ensure we had enough to keep us nourished when the snow
came. What she didn't know was that my father was sow-
ing oats of his own, wandering away from our family.

One Friday, with my father gone for another long winter weekend, we got a foreclosure notice in the mail. He secretly took out a second mortgage on our home and stopped
paying it so he could afford to court another woman. My
mother raged quietly, calling her parents long-distance
from a pay phone to ask if they would loan her money. I
don't remember much of that foreclosure drama, but I do
remember that money was always tight.

Our family rarely went out to dinner. Each time we
traveled to Kingston, a good forty-five minutes away from
our village. Living in the backcountry, we weren't used to
seeing the city lights—Kingston was Las Vegas to me.

On one of our rare outings, we waited in the foyer of a
restaurant, taking in the buzz of voices, transfixed by this
unfamiliar, colorful world. At the table, I struggled with
the huge, plastic-coated menu, nearly knocking over the
tumblers filled with soda, a beverage I'd never tasted. To
me, it was like nectar of the gods.

The arrival of the pizza was majestic. It even had its
own stand. I wanted to dive in, but it was too hot. I waited

impatiently, inhaling the scent of pepperoni, my lips lifting in a pizza-eating smile.

Everything was magic—until the bill came. Maybe it was more than they expected. Maybe it wasn't. "Oops, looks like we'll have to wash dishes." My father winked at me.

We didn't wash dishes that night, but I worried we should have, perhaps because he was once arrested for bouncing a check that paid for a family dinner in a restaurant that looked like a castle. He didn't stop there, either. He pilfered restaurant supplies whenever he could, slipping table settings, glasses, and even platters under his shirt when we were out without my mother. He knew she would never go for that behavior.

Maybe that's why I started plucking the change out of my mother's wallet, quarter by quarter, until my pockets were lumpy with coins. I kept them in my underwear drawer, which rattled each time I opened it. I wanted to be ready for the bus ride home from school, when our driver allowed my brothers and me to get off at the general store for a few minutes while he rambled down a dirt road to drop off two other kids. We had about fifteen minutes to shop in what was nothing more than a shack with a cooler in the back full of milk and shelves lined with sweets and chips.

We were accustomed to once-a-month visits to the grocery store under the watchful eyes of our mother, so we loved having the chance to browse unsupervised. Thanks to the spoils from my mother's purse, I had enough money to stash my backpack full of Hostess Potato Chips in ketchup flavor, a few packets of Smarties, and chewing gum.

It was my belly that gave me away. My mother noticed when it started pushing beyond my waistband. She eventually realized that I was raiding her purse and where the money was going. She talked to the bus driver, and I was left pressing my forehead against the bus window, staring longingly at the store each time we passed. My cheating ways foiled for the time being.

My father's cheating ways continued, however, and as my parents fought, tearing into each other, I'd hide in the pantry, stuffing myself with walnuts and Saltines, trying to ignore the sound of their arguing, trying to fill the hole in my heart. When I turned nine, my mother finally left him and took my brothers and me to Vermont so that she could work as a nurse and finish her degree.

At first, I blamed myself. I thought I wasn't a good enough daughter, and my self-confidence slipped away with each pound I gained. But mostly, I blamed my mother for ripping me from my dad and my home. I've never looked much like my mother: my hair, straight and blonde, hers brown, with a bit of a wave. Other than our wide hips, we didn't have much in common. We were two disconnected beings who came together only during the holidays when she would let me help her make *krumkake,* a Scandinavian cookie served with whipped cream and strawberries.

Looking back, it makes sense that she would have tried to find her own life after leaving my father. She searched for a new boyfriend, finished her nursing degree, and struggled to support us. But I felt as if I'd been shelved along with her erstwhile gardening books. My father visited only once or twice a year and made it feel like we couldn't breathe without his permission. He made it clear that he resented paying for a hotel, though he'd sometimes take my brothers and me out for a meal.

"Bet you don't eat like this with your mother," he said during one visit, directing me toward the steaming Thanksgiving buffet. "Now if only I could afford this with what I'm paying your mother." Too soon, he was gone, leaving me to my latchkey life, dreaming of decadent restaurant meals, wondering if he ate like that without us.

On lonely afternoons after school, I took comfort in making myself Kraft Mac & Cheese. I liked the ritual of it: watching the water boil, turning the steaming pot over into the colander, melting the butter in the hot sauce pan, dumping in the noodles, and stirring in the vibrant orange cheese powder, which clung perfectly to the macaroni. Though the snack relieved my hunger, I still felt empty, inevitably searching for something else to eat. A new boxed cereal was the start of a life-long love affair. I could take handful after handful, robotically reaching into the dark box, even ignoring the prize and instead looking for something to fill my void. I felt lonely, hollow as I navigated the playground crushes of fourth and fifth grade and entered the snake pit that is middle school. No one was there for me. No one except food.

My father's mother, Margaret, felt like the only steady adult presence in my life. Surprisingly, she opted to come along with us to Vermont and lived nearby in a high-rise apartment building on St. Paul Street in Burlington. I thought she was exciting: she'd gotten a facelift many years prior to make sure she could compete with the younger girls in her office, and she painted her lips bright fuchsia with a little brush she carried in her makeup case. When we went out together, she'd wear her finest clothes, which she had sewn herself, and accessorized with clip-on earrings and a matching necklace. We'd walk arm in arm and stop at the deli for meatball sandwiches. She didn't care what I weighed. If I got bigger, she simply made me bigger clothes.

Margaret also struggled with her weight. She was constantly trying to lose ten or twenty pounds and kept a rotating series of diet plans taped to her fridge. They usually involved cottage cheese, grapefruit, and melon. Often, we would eat the prescribed meals together, though she emphatically explained that the diet was for her, not me. Neither of us lost weight.

"You're welcome here at any time," she would say to me as we sat across from each other at her tiny table that was no bigger than a cafeteria tray. Just those words nourished me. I felt safe, warm (she was on the ninth floor of a senior high-rise, so it was like an oven).

As for my mother, she was our family's provider, which meant she spent most of her time at the hospital where she worked as a psychiatric nurse. Her absence left us all vulnerable. My brother Derek buried himself in schoolwork and jobs, from having a paper route to being a grocery cashier, to make extra money, all the while acting like a surrogate dad around the house. My oldest brother, Bryan, gravitated to friends who steered him into dangerous activities, such as raiding parents' liquor cabinets and setting a rack of clothing on fire at the discount store.

On my twelfth birthday, one of Bryan's friends found me in the living room watching MTV. When my brother went upstairs, the boy climbed on top of me, stuck his tongue in my mouth, and put his hand down my pants, grinding away so that I couldn't breathe. There was no one to stop him, no one to notice, and I didn't scream. This teenager had a violent history, and I was afraid of him. I'd seen him beat up both of my brothers, pummel his own sister, and then throw me against the wall. That first time, I managed to get him off me by distracting him. I offered him something to eat, then scrambled up and fled to the pantry, a safe place.

He came to my room two other times, but I barricaded my door with my dresser and eventually told my mother what happened. She called the police, and the boy got sent away for a while; he was never allowed in our home again.

But the experience of having no protection stayed with me so I fortified myself. That summer, I gained forty pounds.

Chris and I met when I was dating a friend of his, who wasn't the best match. But Chris was, so when the friend and I broke up, I stayed in touch with Chris. We went to concerts, hiked, and chatted on the phone.

By then, I didn't have much experience with men, and what I did have wasn't the greatest.

I had lost my virginity in college to Todd, a resident assistant and a well-read poet guy who had a thing for first-timers. That must have been the draw for him, because at age nineteen, I was a 302-pound virgin. After Todd moved on to my next-door neighbor, I fell in love with Drew. We both struggled with weight, him less so than me. I felt like we were the leftovers, matched oddballs, until one night, tipsy and brazen after twenty-five-cent draft night at a local bar, I worked up the courage to make a move and finally kissed him. After a year of dating, I thought we'd be married, so I followed him from Vermont, where he had flunked out of school, down to the Garden State and lived with him in his mother's attic. That's when I met his adventurous friend Chris, who had just returned from five months in Central America. Once I found a job as a live-in nanny, Drew dumped me.

But when I discovered that the Dave Matthews Band was playing nearby on my birthday, I invited Drew, Chris, and two other women friends to the show. Ever since I had turned twelve, the day I was molested, I dreaded my birthday. I wanted to change the dynamic, and if there was anything that could do it, it was the Dave Matthews Band. The music captured me, carried me like few other bands' could.

When we arrived at the hotel near the open-air venue in Connecticut, we made plans for who would sleep where. I would be in the same bed as Drew, though we agreed nothing would happen because we were no longer together. "Don't worry, I won't jump him," I said to Chris as he settled his toiletry bag near the bathroom sink. I loved that he *had* a toiletry bag. My toothbrush was stuck somewhere inside my shoe. I was surely going to need to borrow some of his toothpaste.

Later, as we walked through the tailgaters on the way to the concert, with Dave Matthews blaring from every speaker, Drew was focused on two things: scoring beer and weed. We were running late, and I felt like I was pulling along a toddler distracted by everything from the main objective—going to the concert. After we found our spot, Chris left for a few minutes. "I'm getting a beer; I'll grab one for you," he told me. Drew left our blanket, too, in search of someone with a joint to share, and I was left alone to sit and watch the crowd. Far off, by the stage fence, I noticed Chris talking to a roadie, then handing him a note.

When he returned, we sang along, jamming our hearts out into the sweet June sky. Drew, on the other hand, was having a terrible time. He couldn't find anyone who would share more than a drag of weed, and though we were broken up, I was disappointed. What could be more romantic than an open-air concert under the stars? But Drew wasn't into the music, nor was he into me.

When the concert was over, Chris mentioned the note he had given to the roadie. "It said, 'Please play "Satellite" and say Happy Birthday to Kara.' I can't believe they didn't do it," he said. "The guy said he would give it to Dave."

It was all I could do to stop myself from bursting into happy tears. It was my birthday, and someone had done something nice for me.

A year later, Drew moved to Hong Kong and fell in love with an Austrian woman. Dating each other still wasn't on Chris's or my mind. Chris was seeing a woman two decades his senior, with lots of money to spare, who offered him trips and goodies and even a chance to pursue his life as a novelist. But when things got serious, he backed away. I dated, too, if you could call it that—I was seeing a Scottish guy who, after a few romps, suggested marriage. He was an incredible kisser and his accent shook my knees, but I could see pretty clearly that I was being set up to be used for a Green Card.

I always suspected someone who said they liked me. Were they looking for a quick lay? I had reason to question. There were frat boys who had dared one of their brothers to hook up with me. There was a guy who had kissed me to distract me while his buddies robbed our vacation house. When someone wanted me, they wanted something else because how could they want this body? Over the years, I had blanketed it with fat, distancing myself from others.

Mostly, I avoided dating and spent more time with Chris, excited by his enthusiasm for the outdoors and literature. One weekend, he invited me to come skiing with him and his roommate, Gene, up in the Catskills. Though I'd grown up in Vermont, I never learned how to ski, but I pretended I had some sort of expertise in the sport. Maybe it was my more active lifestyle since meeting him, but I'd dropped almost twenty pounds and was feeling the kind of confidence that comes with fitting into a smaller pant size.

Also, there was something great about being friends with Chris—I didn't have to worry what he thought of my body. I could laugh, fall (which I did often on the ski slope), belch, eat, and wear ugly clothes (I'd show up in ripped jeans and a 3XL plaid fleece) and we'd still have fun. Even if I had the inkling that he was great boyfriend material, I pushed the thought away, afraid to jeopardize one of my life's greatest friendships.

Lines didn't start to blur on the friendship front until my graduation party. In the weeks before, I'd been thinking more and more about how good we were together. How good he was to me. But I was leaving—moving to California in just a few weeks for my first reporter gig. Why didn't I think of this sooner?

He must have felt the same way, because after the party, he ended up sleeping in my bed.

At first I thought it was just because we were drunk. But he had willingly come to my bed. After he settled himself in, took off his glasses, and put them on my nightstand, he turned to me. With the lights off, I said, "Would it be okay if I kissed you?"

I was shocked I said the words, that I was able to say the words. I was shocked his arms so easily and willingly wrapped around my body. I had never been so lovingly caressed before, and every cell in my body wanted to give the universe a collective high five. It was as if my body shot up into the sky like a rocket, emitting rainbows over the entire globe.

Suddenly, I wasn't so afraid of my body. It wasn't

something to hide; it was something that someone *wanted*. I pulled the sheets away from myself as we caressed each other, and we fell asleep in each other's arms.

I went to California, and Chris flew out to visit and I flew home so many times on my puny newspaper salary that the curbside check-in guy remembered my name. I wanted to be near this man I loved, first as a friend, and now with my heart and with my body. Once, we talked about breaking up—because of the distance—but by morning we decided we didn't want to be without each other.

His parents weren't so sure. It wasn't until years down the road that I learned his father had casually mentioned, "You know, there are other fish in the sea." Thin fish is what he meant. Perhaps they didn't think he could love someone my size. But it was serious. And Chris made me feel confident in my own skin.

I bought a new outfit with a short skirt and a pretty, sequined white top to meet him in Las Vegas. I rarely wore white, especially because I had once read it made you look heavier. But everything about Chris made me feel more beautiful. I put on makeup, painted my toenails. I wanted to be his arm candy.

So when Chris and the family traveled to Vegas for their family reunion, I jumped in the car and drove to see him. I arrived to find him, his family, and everyone else lounging by the hotel pool. I hadn't brought a swimsuit.

Actually, I didn't own one. I hadn't been to a pool in years because I was embarrassed about baring my legs and hips. And I couldn't run out and get one, not only because I barely had enough money for gas but also because I didn't know where to find the closest Lane Bryant, probably the only store that would have a suit in my size.

I didn't exactly want to put on a suit in front of his family anyway. So I just dangled my feet in the water, awkwardly pressing my hands back on the concrete patio, trying to relax but feeling very much out of place. Chris playfully splashed me, trying to help me have fun, and even tried to pull me in at one point. I wanted to be playful, too, but I resisted—I didn't want to be drenched, in wet, clinging clothes, in front of his family.

At this first gathering, it felt like no one in Chris's family wanted to talk to me. Maybe they figured I wouldn't be around in Chris's life for much longer. Of course, it could have been because they hadn't seen each other in a long time and were excited to catch up on their own lives. But I felt like an intruder, crashing Chris's reunion. I worried about his parents, that they expected more for their handsome son, their only child. Did they think I would slow him down?

In truth, the two of them were friendly to me, but not warm. His parents were smart and well-off, compared with my scrappy backcountry upbringing and my reclusive dad. I just didn't fit in. Chris's father was a banker, and my father hated bankers, perhaps because he was always indebted to them. His parents intimidated me, and I worried they talked about me the moment I left the room.

What I really cared about, especially during that Vegas trip, was spending time with Chris. After he finished swimming, I pried my thighs, like giant suction cups, off the cement and rushed into the air-conditioned Tropicana Hotel. His room had a mirrored ceiling, which made me very self-conscious.

I wanted to pull the covers over us, but Chris pulled them off. Seeing myself turned me off, so I averted my eyes, or closed them most of the time. When we finished panting and sweating in the air-conditioned room, I pulled the covers back over us, held Chris's hand, and put my head on his chest, listening to his heart beat faster.

I didn't share any of my discomfort with Chris because I didn't want to give him reasons to back out of a relationship I felt was the best I could ever do. The truth is, I didn't want to do better. Chris was amazing.

That afternoon, we never mentioned his family or how they must be feeling about the fact that we'd disappeared. I didn't want to complicate things, didn't want to tarnish the idea that he clearly wanted to be with me. All I knew was that it was lovely to be in his arms, lovely to feel loved.

We spent most of the next day together in his room until it was time for him to hop on a red-eye flight back to New Jersey.

A few months later, I returned to New Jersey to start a new job and moved in to an apartment in Morristown, the next town over from Chris's. By this point, his family could tell I was part of his life, and something in his parents seemed to shift. They tried to get to know me and invited me over on my birthday. Chris's mom had gotten me a lemon cake with a yellow gerbera daisy in the middle. Maybe my moving across the country to be with their son made it clear that I was in his life for good, but all I could wonder was whether his mother had chosen a lemon cake because she thought it was healthier. I was so distracted by this thought that I could hardly enjoy the festivities.

I think it was easier for them—and me—when Chris was accepted into the University of Michigan's business school program, and we moved there together. I got a night job at the nearest newspaper with a job opening—seventy-one miles north of our place in Ann Arbor, a distance I was willing to drive each day, even in Michigan winters, to be with Chris. The position was a step down, but I felt like he and I were starting our real life together.

Little did I know I'd get a boss who belittled me at every turn. If I asked questions, she called me argumentative, and then stuck me with the stories no one else wanted because I was the only reporter on duty at night. Just to cope I had fast food on my desk all night; my keyboard was greasy from the French fries on my fingertips. I'd done well at my other reporting jobs, but I quickly grew flustered with the amount of work coming my way and made mistakes far too often in an industry where accuracy is paramount. Once, I wrote that the governor was committed to "pubic service" instead of "public service."

Oops.

Finally, the executive editor pulled me into his office to talk about how things weren't working out.

"How about we make today your last day?"

I sang at the top of my lungs all seventy-one miles home.

That weekend, Chris suggested we do something special for our anniversary. "Let's see what's going on around here," he said, looking up event listings. We found an international beer festival in Frankenmouth, a German town north of us that was full of cheese shops. We ended the night in a chicken restaurant where the wait staff dressed in full lederhosen—a boisterous tourist stop with surprisingly delicious food.

Chris was uncharacteristically giggly on the way home and held my hand as I drove. I wondered if the beer had gone to his head. When we passed a bridge where a newly married couple posed for photos, I noticed his palm felt sweaty.

Uh-oh, I thought. *He doesn't want to do that anytime soon. I can't even keep a job. Why would he want to marry me?*

But that night in bed, after the lights were out, after I slipped under the covers, he grabbed my hand.

"I was wondering if you'd like to get married," he said.

"Really?"

He pulled out a box, and I felt the velvet in the darkness. It creaked open and, then, a sparkle reflected the light coming in between the curtains. "Will you marry me?"

"Yes, of course. Yes. Yes. Yes."

The night dissolved into a thousand kisses. It was real.

*C*hris's mother, Robin, welcomed us home with an engagement party, and it was beautiful. Chris and I stole glances at each other from across the room while friends toasted our bright future. I felt happy, hopeful. I even wore a light beige linen skirt for the occasion (I rarely wore anything other than black on my bottom half). Afterward, his mom printed out a photo of us that seemed to be stretched out, as if Photoshopped out to make me look taller and leaner. I hoped it was a resizing error.

I spent the summer looking at bride magazines, falling in love with gorgeous dresses, but none that would fit me. I ultimately decided to get a dress at the Filene's Basement wedding sale. I had covered that event in years past for my newspaper and remembered that they had plus-size dresses. That would avoid the whole getting-fitted-for-a-wedding-dress experience. I didn't want my mother and friends standing around me as I tried to find something that fit and covered the burns on my chest.

As we planned our wedding, Chris's parents told us they wanted to pay for our honeymoon. This astounded me, because my own father was complaining about the cost of simply attending the wedding. I thought he would have been over the moon that I was marrying so well, to a loving man and a good family.

Instead of a posh Hawaiian escape, we opted for a two-month around-the-world adventure on $50 a day—four months before the wedding. An early honeymoon, why not? Chris had just finished grad school and hadn't found a job yet, and we agreed that we could always make more money, but we could never make more time. We also told each other it would be the best premarital test, traveling on a dime, staying in hostels, and backpacking our way across continents.

We worked our way around the globe, starting in Brazil at our friends' wedding. Along the way there, we dove into the emerald green ocean, ate seafood, drank *caipirinhas* on a sailboat, and walked among the lush, deep flora that is Rio.

In the Thai islands, I sat with Chris as he played guitar at a $5-a-night beachside resort with only cold-water showers. The humidity made me hot and sticky. We sat on the sand, snorkeled even though I had always been afraid of sharks, got Thai massages. A boy (I assumed he was the Thai woman's grandson) looked with wonder in the massage tent at my large body before retreating to the beach.

We made our way to India and found ourselves on a bus on the way to Agra to see the Taj Mahal, a beautiful marble temple made out of a great love. We were writing our love story—laughing as we met each different character, such as an orange toupee-wearing Mr. Jimmy, who tried to pull us off the bus to lure us into shops. We ignored people staring at such a large creature in their country. It didn't seem to matter to either of us, as we were there to look too. We marveled at the architecture of Jama Masjid, the Red Fort, and Lotus Temple and felt a deep peace when we visited the memorial for Gandhi. We had just four days in the heat of summer—torture for big-bodied folks like me—to see all we could in India, but I didn't wince.

Chris nursed me to wellness after I caught a stomach bug, possibly from eating with wild abandon in India. Then, he fought off advances from a flirty tour guide in the Czech Republic as I recovered. He held my head in his lap on the train ride through the countryside.

When we arrived in Munich, we drank from beer steins the size of our heads in a real *biergarten*. I sighed, to be experiencing life at Chris's side. As tubas oompahed in the shade, the blistering sun made sweat bead on our foreheads, and a waitress in lederhosen plunked down our bratwurst orders with a thud.

We shared a smile as we hefted our steins. *This is what joy looks like,* I thought. The intensity of Chris's eyes, the taste of the beer, the conversation and music. It was all bliss and beauty swirling. I felt like I was in a nineties love movie montage.

We took an all-day walking tour of Berlin. We chased the daylight in the city with a museum pass and ran through seven of the most amazing collections of art and history I'd ever seen. We collapsed in a hostel with Ikea-esque sheets, too tired and too foot blistered to move.

It didn't end there. We sampled chocolate, waffles, and art through Belgium.

In Amsterdam, after a day hunting curiosities, from a giggly walk through the Red Light District to a stop in a cannabis café and a drink at the Heineken factory, we went back to our hotel room. It was there, with the stars surrounding us like a warm blanket and our bodies inter-twined, we made our vows to each other, to be loving and faithful. Tears rolled down my face. From that moment, our souls were intertwined as well.

We ended the trip in Paris by walking up the stairs of the Eiffel Tower together, something I didn't think I'd ever have the daring to do without Chris at my side. Escalators and open-air stairs terrified me. The sun rippled on the

Seine. We walked the Champs-Élysée, without a blister. If I had one, I couldn't feel it—I must have been too happy.

This was love. Love for adventure. Love for each other.

Four months later, we got married in a historic barn in Waitsfield, Vermont, in front of 120 family and friends. We fed each other slices of Ben & Jerry's ice cream cake. My father came after all, but kept to himself; my father-in-law gave a toast about learning to love me as his daughter-in-law. It was beautiful, and to officially be family, I was happier than I'd ever been.

After our wedding, I returned to work and started to diet, cutting out carbs, with Chris cheering me on. I was determined to be the only person who lost weight after the wedding. I wasn't doing it only for me. I was almost thirty years old, and my weight had climbed back above three hundred pounds. I wanted to be healthy for Chris. I wasn't living the life I wanted to be living at that weight.

I'd always gotten adventure travel catalogs in the mail—the kind that offer treks to Macchu Picchu and the Alps. And I'd tell myself that I would go when I lost weight. But I never lost weight. I decided to just start hiking, often with Chris by my side. We made it to the top of Camel's Hump, Vermont's second highest peak; then down—and back up—the Grand Canyon.

Finally, after months of training, we conquered Mount Kilimanjaro. Five and half days up—each step taking

Chris and me closer to death as the oxygen thinned. We helped each other through nausea, sleep deprivation, debilitating headaches, and lack of toilet paper.

A year after we married, I was down 120 pounds. Chris was proud of me. He loved me. I hoped he'd still love me if I gained the weight back.

A year after summiting Kilimanjaro, Chris and I had another adventure in mind, one involving a whole new set of gear, skills, and even a new language. We were going to have a baby.

I worried about what kind of mother I would be. So I did what I always do when I'm anxious: I ate.

"I can't diet right now," I'd tell Chris, who didn't dare comment on whatever I was putting into my mouth, even as the numbers on the scale crept back up past 260, 270, 280, and then 290 all within nine months.

Needless to say, there are no images of me naked in the woods, cradling my pregnant belly under a full bosom in a perfect Demi Moore silhouette. The only photo I could find from my pregnancy with Anna was me at my baby shower, where I look, well, normal. In other words, fat. Cupcakes from Magnolia Bakery in New York City were served. They were the best damn cupcakes I had ever had.

So I had three.

I imagine it must have been a complicated thing, getting sweets for me. A celebration calls for sweets. But buying cupcakes for a pregnant woman who was putting on weight at an unhealthy rate—well, it's tough for me to imagine what went through the minds of my friends and family members as they tried to pick something out, something delicious, but not *too* delicious.

Then there were plus-size maternity clothes, which on me were more like tents, billowing in the breeze and hanging down to mid-thigh. I preferred to wear the yoga pants and baggy shirts I'd favored before I lost weight. I thought I hated my fat clothes, but they were the only thing that I was comfortable in. Good thing I hadn't given them all away because I slowly started to fit in them again.

Perhaps I was betting against myself, as if I knew, deep inside, that my weight loss wouldn't be permanent. Maybe it was that being pregnant felt as if I was losing control of my body, like I did after my assault. Fat was my protection and, as my body felt vulnerable and at the whim of nature while growing another being inside of me, I needed cover.

All told, I put on seventy pounds during that pregnancy. I looked like I did before I dropped more than a hundred pounds. People never offered me a seat on the subway because my baby belly never exceeded my width.

No one reached out and grabbed my belly, like they do to some baby mamas. No one even noticed that I was pregnant until I was eight months along. Instead of being round, my body was a series of lumps. First, my disappointingly small breasts, no larger than a B cup even while pregnant, a predicament in my obese life because many plus-size clothes were designed to accommodate a voluptuous bosom I didn't possess. Adjacent to my teacup breasts were my over-the-bra flab pockets, one on each side. Then, there was a mid-ab layer, where a six-pack typically starts on a fit person, followed by my belly, pooching out like a giant lumpy pillow. Below that, my lower abs nestled beneath a sheet of flab that dangled like an apron, leaving a sweaty, sometimes rash-y spot just above my pubic area. Ugh.

Because no one noticed, I ended up having to tell people I was expecting. Not expecting a sandwich. Not expecting a Frappuccino. Not a Ben & Jerry's Vermonster ice cream sundae with twenty-five scoops of ice cream, cookies, a brownie, whipped cream, and more. . . . Okay, well maybe sometimes I would have expected that. But not this time. I was expecting a baby.

Usually, the announcement was met with a *Wow— how could that have happened?* look, as if my size precludes me from being sexual. I spent years trying to prevent people from thinking I was sexy by adding weight to protect my body. Now I had to explain, one way or another, that I was pregnant, knowing that behind the surprised smiles were thoughts like, "You have sex?" and "How?"

I've asked Chris, at various points in our life together, if guys ever asked him crass questions about having sex with me, of the "Hey, man, how do you do it with her? Are you crushed with her on top?" variety. He assures me they never have, swears up and down. These questions, he tells me, are all in my mind, and maybe they are, because I find myself thinking those kinds of things whenever I see a large person with a skinny partner. Could I help it if I assumed that others wondered the same things?

When the time came to have Anna, I went natural all the way. Despite my size, despite my weight gain, everything from my blood sugar to my blood pressure remained normal. Then on the eve of her due date, after eating smoky corn chowder, I felt a trickle, then a gush. My water broke.

I was ready for labor, my bag packed, loaded with Snatam Kaur yoga music, prepared to give birth without drugs. I'd heard that it was difficult for practitioners to get an epidural right on plus-size people. I was no medical doctor, but I imagined bulges of fat obscuring the anesthesiologist's vision and steering the needle away from my spinal cord and into a kidney (even if that is anatomically impossible). Also, I hated the idea of a needle in my back.

I'd used food to avoid emotional pain for most of my life, at great cost. But when it came to giving birth, I looked the prospect of pain straight in the eye, grunted, screamed, and gave it a standing fuck-you. I was going to feel the pain of a cantaloupe-sized head squeezing through my lady parts without the benefit of painkillers—or food, because I wasn't allowed to eat. There I was, fully, painfully present and hungry, ready to bear down and have my daughter.

Maybe I was motivated by the thought of my mother giving birth to me and my brothers naturally, before such things were done. If she could do it, so could I.

And so, Chris and I walked the hospital halls. I bounced on a big, *big* rubber ball. We listened to yoga meditation music. And it was all fine, for the first hour or two.

But I was only dilated three centimeters out of the ten required. My contractions were like tiny little cramps up to the twenty-second hour, when my doctor told me that I had to give birth within two hours or she'd take me in for a C-section. Reluctantly, I opted for Pitocin, a drug used to speed up contractions. Without an epidural, it felt like I'd been injected with rocket fuel, the contractions suddenly coming hard and fast, a 7.0 earthquake on the contraction scale. Chris fed me ice chips, the only thing I knew to ask for as I writhed into full-throttle labor. My eyes tilted upward like some possessed demon's, and my hair strewed out like Medusa's snakes after I pulled at it, trying to disperse the pain.

Little Anna was born less than an hour later at 11:31 p.m.

She was tall like me, and perfect on the weight charts. That's the way I wanted to keep her. Perfect.

Her birth was the first time I'd seen my emotional rock of a husband cry.

"She's hungry," a nurse said, and handed me the tiny swaddled bundle that was my daughter. I felt a wave a fear as I held her in my arms, but when I pressed her against my breast, she immediately latched on.

And I was feeding my child.

I wasn't very good at feeding myself, and I wasn't sure how to do it right for her, but she knew what she was doing. In the coming weeks, it was clear that Anna loved to nurse, and I loved to nurse her. As exhausting as it was to be a milk wagon, I loved providing something as simple and true as her first nutrients.

My milk was, of course, laced with everything I ate, including a surfeit of sugar. As she nestled against me, her little lips sucking, I sometimes worried that I'd already ruined her by feeding her too often, or by giving her my DNA. Was I feeding her all that I was? Had I already given her my flawed genes? Maybe, if she was lucky, she'd end up with more of Chris's genes than mine.

I didn't want Anna to ever struggle like I had. I didn't want her ever to feel abandoned or demoralized. I didn't want her to feel emotionally hungry. I didn't want her to have the wrong clothes. The wrong friends. The wrong boyfriends.

The wrong body.

Anna was born in February, when the temperature was so cold your eyelids froze. Home from the hospital, I assumed Chris and I would hunker down with our baby to keep her warm and safe. But after a few days of this, cabin fever set in. The floors were too creaky. The doors were too drafty. And Chris was going stir crazy.

"So, I was thinking about going for a hash run," he said. To the uninitiated, a hash run is a run with a running group, otherwise known as drinkers with a running problem. Someone goes ahead to set up a trail, marking it with flour and chalk for the group to follow, with a false clue or two thrown in for good measure. It's all good fun, especially because they sing dirty ditties and drink a lot.

I wasn't going to be one of those wives who made her husband stay home just because she had to. "Sure. Have fun," I said. I was still in sitting-on-an-ice-pack-post-birth mode.

As soon as Chris left, I went to the basement with the load of laundry, ignoring the fact that I wasn't supposed to lift anything heavier than twenty-five pounds. As I climbed back up the stairs, out of shape and hovering around three hundred pounds, I felt my episiotomy stitches pull. Panicked, I grabbed the stair railing and hoisted myself up the rest of the way, stepping onto the wood floor of our living room with an earsplitting *creak*. One load of laundry, one flight of stairs, and I felt faint and was slick with sweat.

The loud creak woke Anna and she began to cry. I couldn't decide who to take care of first, her or me.

"Just a minute, sweetie. Mommy will be right there."

I swooped in her room, feeling a bit dizzy and nauseated. Meanwhile, my breasts were bursting as I picked up my wailing daughter, then sat down on our blue floral garage sale couch. The seat sagged when I landed, and I felt another pulling on the stitches. Anna continued to wail.

"Shhh, sweetie," I said. I said it again and again and again. But she wouldn't stop until I put her to my breast. Sometimes, she drifted off to sleep, but I couldn't stand up without waking her, and eventually, my need to go to the bathroom became urgent.

I was stuck.

Chris's hash runs were maybe four or five hours long. By now, his buddies were probably congratulating him over a beer for being a new father. I wanted to be happy for him, wanted to seem like I had it all together, but when Chris returned smelling of alcohol, I smelled of blood, urine, sour breast milk, and meconium, the black, sticky, tar-like baby poop that had smeared on me somewhere. I was more splotched, stained, and smelly than I had ever been in my life.

Chris kept his distance, knowing that postpartum hormones were surging through my body. But I tried to act normal and didn't complain, not then, and not over the next few weeks despite my sleep deprivation and soreness from childbirth. Through it all, I kept quiet, hiding my feelings. I soothed myself with food, crunching away any complaints or cries for help with handful after handful of cereal, swallowing my frustration when he turned up the volume on his favorite TV show because Anna was crying and he couldn't hear.

That's not to say Chris wasn't a great dad—he was. He worked hard to provide for us, feeling even more pressure to do so while I was out on maternity leave. When he was home, he changed diapers and read to Anna every night, soothing her with passages from *Charlotte's Web* and *Stuart Little.* The stories didn't put Anna to sleep, but I'd nod right off, propped up on pillows against our headboard.

Soon, Anna was crying and I was awake again. I would have loved to give Chris a chance to feed the baby at night, but any time I pumped, there was just a trickle of breast milk, not enough for a baby. Besides, he didn't wake up when she cried at night. Without sleep, I was incapable. Everything was difficult—talking, breathing, thinking, loving.

I felt isolated, but food kept me company, and it was easier to hide what I was eating if I was always alone.

As I adjusted to becoming a mother, I tried very hard to be a part of the real world, a part of Chris's world. To get up and have breakfast with him, to have a conversation. To pretend I was his partner, even with my stain-covered clothes, even though I smelled. But I felt Chris wanting to escape. I didn't blame him. But I didn't say anything because I didn't want him to go.

I wanted to escape, too. I had taken four months of maternity leave, and when the reality of returning to work and the cost of child care hit me, I opted to work from home. I figured I'd work while the baby slept, never suspecting that sleep and Anna didn't get along.

Feeding her allowed us both to get some rest.

I'd sworn to nurse her exclusively, not least because I'd heard that nursing helped a mother lose weight and reduced a child's risk of obesity. And I was terrified that Anna would be obese, like me. Years before I got pregnant, I saw a talk show featuring an eighty-pound four-year-old. I was horrified and worried at the same time. Would that be my child?

And so, at the beginning, I nursed all the time. She wailed when I pulled her away just for a moment to use the bathroom or to get a drink of water or to shake out my legs, numb from sitting and nursing all day.

It turns out that I was a low breast milk producer, but I was reluctant to supplement because the lactation consultants had told me that if I did, my supply would decrease even more. Plus, we couldn't afford to buy formula. Instead, I found money for herbal concoctions to increase my milk and that made my sweat smell like maple syrup. And so, Anna was hungry. She didn't sleep for more than two hours at a stretch until we started introducing solid foods when she was four months.

My life went on this way for ten months, until I finally broke down and found a day care that I could afford in the next town over. For the first week, I returned home and crawled into the fetal position, unsure of what to do with the sudden quiet time. I'd dreamed of being productive or, at least, social, but often, I did nothing or spent hours scrolling through Facebook, taking voyeuristic pleasure in other people's lives to distract me from my own mess.

I needed to start taking care of myself again, but I was caught in a monsoon of guilt. I didn't spend these expensive free hours exercising; instead, I used the quiet time to eat whatever we had in the house, even if it was just clumpy brown sugar from a box. The scale became obsolete. As with a mousetrap, where you want to catch the mouse but are horrified to glance down and see it gored by the copper hinge, I needed to look at the scale but was afraid to.

Part of taking care of myself meant getting out in the world and moving—and I tried. I walked when I could, rambling around the neighborhood with Anna in her stroller, trying to keep up a pace that might pass as exercise. But it wasn't much. So when my friend Jessica asked me to do the Emerald Nuts Midnight Run, a four-mile race in Central Park, I said yes. It started at the stroke of midnight on the first of January, with fireworks and nonalcoholic Champagne stops throughout the course. It sounded fun and adventurous.

And cold. On January 1, the wind howled and flapped the shrubs against the siding of our home. The Weather Channel reported forty-mile-an-hour gusts and a wind chill of below zero.

Chris's look said, "Are you sure you want to go out there?"

I was.

Anna was ten months old and I was still wearing maternity clothes. Worse, I wasn't my old adventurous self anymore. Two years earlier, I'd trekked to the summit of Mount Kilimanjaro to celebrate a 120-pound weight loss. Now, I spent my days circling my kitchen, looking for food. I was lost within my own six-foot-tall, three-hundred-pound body, too big not to notice but invisible just the same.

Going out into the cold felt like a way to take better care of myself. And I could help others, too—I had decided to use the event to raise funds for UNICEF. Still, that didn't mean I was ready. I had done some jaunts on the treadmill, though nothing close to four miles. But I went. Sure, I didn't run, or even jog. It was more like a galumphing walk. But I did it.

The point was the challenge. I was mired in despair and wanted to change, and walking through Central Park at midnight woke my urge to do something about it.

In the weeks after the race, I noticed just how stuck I was between intention and action. I bought diet books only to let them collect dust on the shelf. I vowed to drink just protein shakes, then ended up slurping them down as a snack in addition to everything else I ate and drank. I paid a weekly fee for one weight loss group or another, then neglected to follow the program. That all had changed when I was training for Mount Kilimanjaro that first time—when I had a challenge as enormous as the weight of my body.

I decided to end the new year by climbing Mount Kilimanjaro *again,* scaling to the summit once more to gain control of the scale, to gain control of my life. I wasn't ready for it—I'd have to train. And to motivate me through the training, I made my effort a fund-raiser. Each month,

I signed up for a different event, from a 5K for the Goodwill Rescue Mission in Newark, New Jersey, to a walk for multiple sclerosis around a zoo in Tampa, Florida. I got a lot of blisters and a drawer full of free T-shirts. But the experience made me feel brave, as if, for once, losing weight was beside the point. I was out of the house. I was moving. I was alive.

Of course, unlike 5Ks, bike rides, or a jump in the lake, climbing Kilimanjaro isn't something you just *do*. It takes preparation and prowess. I knew that, and still, I put off doing the things I needed to do to train for the hike, such as, you know, hiking. I told myself I was good in high altitude. That it was just a slow walk to the top. That my binge eating didn't matter because at least I'd been moving.

But it did matter. I was doing it every day, every hour, standing with my fleshy back against the freezer door as I ate straight from a carton of ice cream that was meant for my husband's dessert, my problems melting away, sweet and creamy like Breyer's Vanilla.

Each day, as I "trained" for my second Kilimanjaro try, I balanced out my workouts with something big and crammed with calories, like homemade mac and cheese cooked up with Gruyere and Vermont white cheddar. I made high-calorie dishes for any occasion—when a neighbor was having foot surgery or another had suffered a death in the family—then whipped up one for us at the same time, nibbling away as I went and eating most of the leftovers.

When it came time to pack for that second trek up the mountain, I was in such denial about my eating habits and my body that I packed the same stuff I'd worn for my first trek—when I was seventy pounds thinner. It did not occur to me that I'd done this until I was in the hotel room the night before the climb. My "skinny" pants would not budge over my hips, and I had to ask the hotel clerk to find someone to turn my two pair of hiking pants into one gargantuan pair. I consumed a few pounds of candy while I waited for the tailor to do his work.

I hiked the mountain as if I were wearing cement hiking boots.

I didn't make it to the summit. Not even close.

I didn't have the Oprah-esque *aha* moment I'd hoped for. Instead, I went home and binged myself off a cliff.

By the time Anna was two years old, we finally ditched her bottle. I told her that the bottle fairy had come to take it to another baby who needed it. She seemed okay with this but subsequently lost all interest in drinking milk. So, of course, I told the pediatrician.

"Try chocolate milk," she said. "I'd much rather have her drinking chocolate milk than juice. At least there are nutrients in the milk. Juice is mainly sugar," she explained.

That night, I bought chocolate milk. It went over very well. "Chocolate milk. Chocolate miiiiiiiiiiiilk," Anna cried whenever we passed a cooler in a grocery store or pharmacy aisle. I felt the other customers looking at me. "The pediatrician told us that it's healthier than juice," I explained, though no one had asked.

I worried that people would think I was poisoning my own child, or, at least, making her as fat as I was. I felt the need to apologize to these strangers, for myself, my lack of self-control on display for all to see, and for my daughter.

Except I didn't need to apologize. Anna was getting the calcium she needed. I was being a good mom, even if no one thought so.

So why couldn't I be a good mother to myself? Why was I able to make decent decisions for Anna (even if others looked askance) yet stuff myself with crap food? I had enough guilt for both of us, apparently. Often, I found myself noticing what Anna was eating at a party, and noticing what others were noticing. Even if another child was raiding the cookie tray, I tried to cap the number of confections Anna consumed in a sitting, partly for her health but also for the perception other people had about her health.

Maybe I couldn't stand to observe her child-like impulses, the crying out for chocolate milk or the grabbing of sweets at a party, as if those impulses were not hers but mine. The truth was, I could control her, but I couldn't control myself. Every bite I took shaped my fat, shaped my body.

But I had created Anna's body. It's possible, I tell myself, that I can shape a better life for her. Maybe it will be easier for her to start when she is at a healthy size than to work backward, trying to undo every bite or slurp that could lead to a three-hundred-pound-plus body like mine.

What I didn't want to do was create a monster, a dieting-obsessed, confidence-lacking monster. I wanted to create a girl who was proud of who she was, who had unshakable love for herself whatever she decided to do in life. A girl in tune with her body, who ate when she was physically hungry, not emotionally hungry.

Was I, at my size, showing her that this was the way she should be? Or was I showing her what she didn't want to be? I fervently hoped it was the latter.

Fast forward a few years, as I stood in line at the bakery, Anna smearing her mouth and fingers across the glass case of cookies, I had a moment of clarity: *This was my idea.*

We didn't have time for breakfast I had told myself before we left the house. But we did have time for a stop at the bakery. I wanted a bear claw, an almond paste confection worth at least five hundred calories. I had been thinking about one since the moment I'd opened my eyes, so I had devised a plan that, because Anna was a good listener while we were getting ready to leave, we should stop at the bakery on the way to school.

She ordered a cinnamon roll larger than her hand, and then filled the back seat with crumbs as she munched it. I told her to dust the crumbs off her sweater so no one saw them.

Oh, no, I thought, *am I teaching her to be clean and presentable or to hide her eating?*

I shouldn't have taken her to the bakery. Or should I? Is it a crime to go to the bakery every once in a while?

Shouldn't that be allowed? Why couldn't I just be someone who simply went to the bakery, got something to eat for myself (and my daughter), and it was no big deal?

Maybe because, for me, there are no good decisions to be made there—between the freshly buttered rolls and the famous Philadelphia Fluff cake or the tarts, beautifully backlit in the curved glass of the cake display. Like a museum exhibit or an upscale jewelry store, the top of the case is polished stainless steel, with just enough room for a cake or tart to be set on top, boxed, and slipped into a fancy handle bag bearing the bakery's Italian name, well known in my neighborhood.

I thought of how silly it must look, me standing in front of the display case of treats, my bottom and hips silhouetted by the light, framed by tarts and the lemon meringue pie that Anna convinced me to buy. I'd tried to make one at home once, but the lemon never gelled and we ended up with a nasty soup below a cloud of fluff. From then on, Anna made me promise to buy lemon meringue pie, not make it. Of course, I agreed, though I tried to teach Anna that this wasn't an everyday occurrence but a special treat.

When I learned I was pregnant with our second daughter, Anna was four years old, and I was terrified. I hadn't lost the weight from my first pregnancy, and I didn't think my body could sustain any more pounds.

I had just started a new, fun job working as a marketing coordinator for a branding firm in New York City. The people I worked for were my dear friends. They allowed me to work from home when necessary. I hated having to ask for an extra-wide chair so my hips wouldn't be pinched, though my boss-friend ordered one for me without hesitation, sweetly reassuring me that it wasn't the first time an employee had needed an accommodation. Who would want to jeopardize a job like that?

At first, we kept the pregnancy news quiet. I sat through a tequila tasting trying to make sure people didn't notice that I didn't do any tasting. I certainly didn't want anyone to say, "Don't worry, you're eating for two."

The second time around, I put on only fifteen pounds, all of it baby and water weight. Fifteen pounds was the maximum I could gain because at three hundred pounds I was considered morbidly obese.

And I finished where I started on the scale, and was determined to go down from there.

Because of my job in the city, I signed Emily up for day care when she was eight weeks old. I had no illusions about trying to work with her in the house. I knew I needed to get out and about. I was determined to get enough help to get me through that first year.

Still, even with help, my life—working, commuting, getting up in the middle of the night—fell apart quickly. My only downtime was binging on *Property Brothers* or *Love It or List It* episodes I'd DVRed while feeding Emily in the dark morning hours.

Feeding myself became a constant contradiction—a battle over what I should or shouldn't have. In my mind, I should have been able to have everything. Eat what you want, some compulsive-eating experts tried to teach me. My body didn't know how full felt. My body wanted everything. Mostly, though, it was all a blur. A big fat blur of food and fury as I tried to keep up with the speed of life.

I was hungry while nursing, which led me to binge, so I started a low-carb diet. I ended up hungrier, despite allowing myself extra calories for breastfeeding. And then it was over before it began. I had a history of blowing it when it came to diets. Maybe that's obvious.

I was tired. So I filled up on caffeine—Frappuccinos with plenty of sugar, which fed my anxiety and gave me a sugar-and-caffeine-pumped rush, necessitating a doughnut on the side just to come down from the ceiling.

I am not one of those people who say they've tried everything.

Sometimes, I just stopped trying.

After that fateful doctor's visit when we received the news that Anna was considered slightly overweight, my kitchen felt like a fish-stick-and-chicken-nugget factory, with cheese pizza on the side. The cold from the freezer blew in my face when I looked in it for something healthy. I needed to make a change but didn't know where to start.

My first official diet had been in middle school, the year after I was sexually assaulted and gained so many pounds. The guy got sent away, and I was forever changed. In addition to the weight gain, I contracted shingles, a virus related to chickenpox but much more painful and normally a risk for elderly or very, very sick adults. The sores ran up and down my spine, hot buttons to my nervous system. My brothers thought it was funny to smack me there, which sent me to the roof in pain.

Later that year, after my shingles scars had healed, my mom took me to Weight Watchers. Snow covered the icy parking lot and seeped into the cracks of my faux leather boots, making them feel tight on my feet, much like how the rest of my clothing felt. I had inherited my mother's feet, with a second toe longer than the big toe, and all the long, skinny digits wanted to curl under in the chill.

Head down, face tucked into my scarf, I shuffled through the slush to the door, yanked it open against the rushing wind, and almost hit my mother in the face. Inside, I saw dozens of middle-aged women with jackets hanging off the backs of their chairs, zipping up their boots after their turn on the scale.

When it was my turn, I didn't want to see the number. I'd avoided the scale since being publicly weighed in sixth grade by the gym teacher, the same woman who handed out tampon sample packs in public. After everyone had a turn, she had announced that I was the heaviest girl in class. I weighed in the triple digits, one-twenty, which seems like a small number now, but then most of my classmates still hovered around the eighty-pound mark. I was carrying around so much more.

That cold and icy night, I was the only kid at Weight Watchers.

Afterward, we shopped for food to fit the plan. For my mom, that meant cantaloupe and cottage cheese, the perfect diet foods. Just eating cottage cheese meant that I was on a diet, that I was eating the "right" way. Later in life, I discovered Oprah's Boot Camp diet, which meant giving up the "white stuff," a.k.a. all refined carbohydrates, and working out eight times a week. I seriously dropped pounds, and then, like with any diet I tried, gained them all back.

When I had my own family, I went through a frozen meals phase, with food delivered each week in a big Styrofoam container. I'd make my family a real meal, something far more delicious, then eat something awful off a black plastic tray. I felt like an outcast at my own table.

After Anna's doctor's appointment, I bought some books on clean eating. After I read them, I cleared my cabinets and freezer, filling two giant garbage bags with everything that contained sugar or fat. Then I headed straight to Whole Foods to restock my kitchen with real food that would nourish me and my girl's body and soul.

Because I was making chili for dinner that night, I decided it would be best to do so with grass-fed ground beef, the healthiest option from a fancy organic market. Then I discovered that the sausage, beef, and fixings for one big pot of chili cost $75—half my grocery budget for the week. Everything healthy seemed double the price of food at our local grocery store, from beans to tomato sauce.

By the time I got to the cash register and shelled out more than $300 for a few days' worth of dinners, my organic food kick had fizzled. The goods may have been sustainable, but not for my budget. Maybe I was blaming money when I should have been blaming myself. I did tend to be an all-or-nothing kind of person. Give me anything labeled *fat-free* and I'd eat it, including Twizzlers and candy canes.

I didn't want my daughter to think of food in terms of right or wrong, fat-free or full-fat. I wanted her to be able to love food. To bite into a homemade brownie and experience its crunch against the warmth of the ooey-gooey center. To linger over a bowl of tapas, engaged in conversation, instead of thinking, *This will never be enough.*

The only time I enjoyed food was when I ate with someone. With company, I could really taste the ingredients, savor the art and care put into a lemon bar or delight in a perfectly cooked and seasoned steak. Eating alone, in my car or at the kitchen counter late at night, I was lost in the vortex of a binge, a vacuum cleaner sucking up everything in sight and still coming up empty.

With a child who was overweight, I had failed as a mother. Anna wasn't born fat. I was feeding her too much. I didn't know the meaning of the word *enough,* so how could I teach it to her? Even on good days when I found time to exercise, to make a salad and eat it, I was constantly in conflict: trying to be at peace with my body while wanting to drop pounds to be healthier. Why did I need to drop pounds if I was already at peace?

Of course, I wasn't at peace, and having a daughter who would struggle like me was my worst nightmare. Too often, my diet attempts came from a place of hating my body, of being utterly sick of myself, inside and out. That's when I would search the internet for a detox diet and find myself whipping up a kale smoothie. Trouble was, I didn't like drinking kale. To me, green drinks tasted a lot like a lawn, as if you'd taken a mouthful of dirt and were about to chomp a blade of grass. Yes. That's the flavor.

My daughter was beautiful, even if she was slightly heavier than what the doctor considered a healthy weight.

I was not beautiful.

I was a beast. An obese beast. I'd gotten myself so fat that it was hard to tell where my body began and ended. My hips, especially, were outlandish, knocking things over as I passed. Sometimes, I couldn't even tell, as if I'd lost the ability to feel my edges. Like Saturn's rings, my hips brought my body into a whole new dimension.

I had once heard that men were instinctively attracted to women with wide hips. Their nature thinks this meant these women would bear healthy, smart children because wide hips can accommodate children with big heads and big brains. But, in reality, I always felt like an unwanted ugly duckling, even when Chris loved me.

So much for being a body-loving being, wishing only good things for my thighs, like we were taught in yoga class. If I could, I would have taken a hedge trimmer to them and shaved them off, along with the apron of fat below my belly, the flaps of skin that were my arms.

With all these extra appendages, it was hard to look normal in anything. Even if I lost weight, I wouldn't look normal. I would be disfigured—stretched and saggy in the places that had stored my excess pounds. I would go from feeling like an eighty-year-old to looking like one.

Could I possibly accept that this was me? And if I accepted it, did that mean I had to stop trying to change? Did it mean I had given up? Did body acceptance mean that I was a failure?

And what of my daughters? If I was who I was, fat and all, then wasn't I demonstrating to my daughters that this was the way a woman should be? Then again, hiding my eating from them wasn't exactly healthy either. They saw the results of my overeating, past and present. Their mother was the fat mom.

In the spring, my friend Sheila told me a community garden was planned for a plot of land about a block from my house. I admired Sheila, a single mom with two beautiful girls. She found time to write, make homemade gifts, and truly listen to her friends. Some of the things she had heard me talk about, again and again, were my struggle with food and my mother's garden.

This garden—with forty-four rectangular, wood-edged plots—was funded by a Centers for Disease Control grant to combat obesity and encourage a healthier way of living. A few days later, as the girls and I turned the corner, heading toward what was once a vacant lot, we saw what Sheila had been talking about. The lot was no longer vacant but more of a construction site, with volunteers sawing lumber into perfect four-by-eight slabs.

I found Sheila and her daughter Evy filling in the soil of their plot.

"Come on, Anna," Evy said, pulling her hand. They immediately walked up the pile of dirt as if scaling a mountain.

"These are for you," said a volunteer, approaching them with two kid-sized shovels. The girls took them and went straight to the edge of the dirt pile. They carried a cup or two of soil with each shovelful but dropped a good half of it between the pile and the plot.

One of the volunteers asked if I was signed up. "No, but I'd like to try it," I said. "My mom was a gardener. I suppose I have it in me to be one, too."

"Looks like we have a few plots left," she said, looking down at her sheet. "You can have number 23."

A garden plot.

It was a few weeks until my thirty-ninth birthday, and with a nine-month-old and a five-year-old, I struggled simply to climb stairs because arthritis had settled into my right knee and the rest of my joints cried for mercy.

But there was hope in this garden, and I took to it with the same kind of enthusiasm I'd felt at the start of so many diets.

After my next paycheck, Anna sat on my lap as we ordered fancy tomato plants and seeds online for kaleidoscope carrots, beans, watermelon, and bell peppers. "Now, remember, if we grow them, we have to eat them," I reminded her. This was a real concern because on more than one occasion she had told me, "I'm allergic to salad."

Worse than that, I'd been relying on plopping her in front of the television while I got my work done. I hoped our community garden plot would be a reason for us to get outside together.

One evening, we took a break from the screen. I pulled out some graph paper because I remembered that my mother had used it to map out her garden. Then I pressed a pen down on the paper, measured out a twelve-by-four garden, and imagined where everything would go. Carrots could be planted sixteen per square foot. Cucumbers and tomatoes needed two square feet each. I scrunched my nose, trying to work out as many vegetable combinations as possible.

I thought about the things I *wanted* to eat. I thought about the things I *should* eat. I thought about what would make me look good as a gardener, with all those other people surveying the fruits of our labor. I plotted it all out, first with pencil, then with a Sharpie, outlining the edges of our space and playing with possibilities.

Anna's eyes lit up when I showed her the garden map. She brought over a tray of fruit-scented markers.

"Now draw sixteen carrots here," I said, pointing to the carrots' spot.

She drew seventeen little orange sticks, allowing for an extra seed. Suddenly, we weren't working on nutrition; we were doing math and art. Vegetable by vegetable, she added to the map, embellishing with swirling vines extending in all directions.

Inspired by her colors, I picked seeds for tomatoes in every hue—Tangerine, Sweet Red, and Solar-Powered varieties. I imagined a tomato and mozzarella salad beaming like a rainbow. I pictured acorn squash, like my mother used to make when I was a kid, with butter, brown sugar, and sage melted in a scooped-out half.

It was such a delicious and warm memory, I wanted us to make our own.

I found seeds for lemon cucumbers and radishes that would grow white on the outside and red on the inside. Whatever colorful or unusual varieties were available, I wanted them, like Martha Stewart meets Frankenstein.

Then we got to planting, starting with the package of radishes the garden committee had given us just for signing up. They spilled all over the place. Although I was looking forward to tight little rows, I was going to have to accept a little messiness.

After planting came waiting. In my life of immediate gratification through food, waiting was agony. It hit me hard.

The thing about depression, I had discovered, was that it ruined everything before it even got started. Something may begin as a dream, but depression makes you map out every possible negative outcome in your mind, and you are thrust into that disaster in the middle of the night, like an express train crashing into a brick wall. This is where every project gets stalled. Every activity. Every diet.

I wondered if my mind worked against me, setting such grandiose expectations that I never seemed to fulfill because I didn't have the money, time, or wherewithal.

Maybe nothing would grow in our garden. Maybe all of it would grow but nothing would change.

I felt embarrassed, and guilty, when the tiny plants in Burpee Seed Company boxes arrived. I remembered that the order had cost more than $100. I tucked the receipt deep down in the recycling bin so my husband Chris wouldn't see it.

Not that he would have minded. I was the one who wasn't used to spending a lot of money. When we needed shoes, he took me to a shoe store in Summit, where stilettos gleamed in the window and cost $300. This wasn't Payless. But my weight required more support than what Payless could offer.

I couldn't wear heels, but I snuck a glance at them longingly before moving on to find something flat and sturdy. In fancy New York City, I wore sneakers with slacks to walk the five blocks from Penn Station to my office, but every step was grueling, the balls of my feet burning, as if the sidewalk was covered in broken glass. I bought myself a good pair of shoes. Not fancy French designer heels with sleek red soles but shoes that helped me walk without pain.

All that money for almost-orthopedic shoes, and I wasn't even forty years old.

When our first crop—radishes—started to pop, their red tops crested the soil and their leaves stretched up like arms begging for someone to pick them up. Anna yanked a fuchsia root right out of the ground, ran to the garden faucet to clean it, and stuck it in her mouth.

"Yum, radishes," she said. I shuddered to think how bitter it must have tasted, but when I chopped some for our salad that night, I put a piece in my mouth. It was sweet and lovely, especially so because we grew it.

Since I signed up on site, I'd picked out our seeds before I knew what was allowed. For example: some plants such as strawberries and mint weren't allowed because they were invasive. I thought it would be fun, if not somewhat magical, to plant pumpkins and winter squash, two of my favorite flavors, along with a little watermelon nestled in with the tomatoes. Knowing that I would have limited space, I selected the Sugar Baby watermelon, which is supposed to be great in containers. I thought it would fit nicely in the garden.

That was until I learned watermelon wasn't allowed because, like winter squash, it had a reputation of taking over a plot with its enormous growth.

It would have to stay my secret.

Hiding food was my downfall, but in this case, I wasn't being "bad." I was trying to be good—to grow something healthy. I hoped that I wasn't transforming watermelon and pumpkin into forbidden foods. There were already too many shouldn'ts in my life—carbs, éclairs, anything with puff pastry. Hopefully, I would get a pass when it came to watermelon because it was a sweet but healthy fix, something that I could share with my family. I let the tomatoes grow around the melon plants, noting a tiny little watermelon bud swelling on the vine.

The question was, What would I do when it got bigger?

Isn't that the problem with all lies and half-truths? The more secret I was with food, the bigger I became.

I had banned things from our house—Barbies, because they promoted poor body images, and Fruit Loops, because they didn't contain fruit—arbitrary rules that I made up to (hopefully) save my daughters from repeating my history with food. Still, life has a way of getting around the rules. Like the day my mother-in-law brought over a bag of clothes for Anna. When I pulled out a cupcake shirt, I immediately thought, "Oh, no."

There it was—a sweet little confection sewn onto a shirt, and a new shirt at that, not one from the thrift store or another kid's outgrown castoffs. I couldn't let her wear this cupcake shirt in public, though it was adorable: a cartoonish rendering with a cherry on top and icing floating off the edges. The muffin tin paper was striped in perfect pink and green. The shirt was a soft petal pink with ruffled sleeves and had matching green shorts. If Anna had a normal-sized mother, this cupcake shirt would have been fine, but she didn't. I worried other mothers would think I was enabling her, embedding sweets in her life and ruining her for good.

One day we sat on a shaded bench while Anna and I enjoyed a rare hot dog from a lunch cart. (I still feel compelled to tell you that we don't eat them much. Really.) I kept one hand on Anna to make sure she didn't launch forward with excitement over her treat. I used my other hand to shimmy my hotdog, donned in ketchup and relish, out of the bag and field Anna's requests to open her water bottle and cheese curls, which stained her fingertips and lips orange for the rest of the day.

An old lady, who must have been about eighty and no more than eighty pounds, looked me up and down, then huffed, glaring at our hot dogs. She stared pointedly at my daughter, then at her hotdog. Then she looked straight in my eyes and shook her head.

I felt like saying, "Lady, I get it. You think I'm making my daughter as fat as I am."

Which is why I could not let Anna wear the cupcake shirt while she was with me. Instead, I saved it for days she spent around the house or with her grandmother.

Not all food clothing was forbidden. Once I had gotten her a pumpkin onesie (size six months, which she wore at three months because she was so tall). I figured a pumpkin was healthy enough. Sweet pea would have been okay, too. But not *sugar, sweetie pie, cream puff,* or any of those deliciously cute food nicknames we give to little girls and, sometimes, grown women. No, those were off the table. And off my daughter.

*W*e were packing up all our winter clothes, our books and bills, stowing them in bins and tucking them in the basement. Our summer clothing, we took with us. We were set to spend the summer living at Chris's parents' house to watch their cats. That way, we could earn a little money renting out our place and spread out in a little extra space at their place.

But there was a little bit of overlap. Chris's parents hadn't left for their farm in Indiana yet and our tenant had already moved in, so we settled in at the bigger house while his parents were still there.

On our first night there with Chris's folks, we learned that James Gandolfini had died from a heart attack at age fifty-one. He was a legend in New Jersey, so my Facebook feed exploded when the news hit, all of us feeling as if we'd lost an extended family member. When Chris and I had lived in Michigan, we inevitably spent Sunday nights watching the latest episode of *The Sopranos* and eating a creative new pasta dish. The routine felt like home, despite the show's crazy storyline.

Earlier that week, my cousin-in-law Troy had dropped to the ground at the RV dealership where he worked, but he survived. I proclaimed that because both Gandolfini and my cousin were smokers, that explained their misfortune. Of course, both were also quite heavy.

My father had his first heart attack when he was thirty-one, and then two others down the road. I was nearly thirty-nine years old, and suddenly my heart felt like a ticking time bomb.

That night, when Chris came upstairs, he told me he'd had a talk with his mother. She said, with news of the actor's heart attack, she felt a new urgency. "What can we do to support Kara, to help her with her weight?" he relayed, as if glad to have an entry to the conversation.

Chris was timid to talk about my weight. The only time he ever made a comment was in jest when he noticed food was missing, a simple, "Ah-ha." Perhaps his reluctance was my fault. I exploded when he bought me a healthy mantra book for my birthday. But I could ask him for a yoga mat in lieu of candy for Easter. As long as I brought up weight, it was okay. If he brought up weight, and I wasn't ready to talk about it, I would blow up or dissolve in tears. But mostly I was a people pleaser, assuring him that everything was okay, I had it under control, and here was my plan.

This time, I said nothing but glanced at the *New Abs Diet* cookbook sitting next to the bed. I liked the smoothie recipes but didn't follow anything else on the plan. I felt hurt and upset that they'd been talking about me behind my back. But would I have rather they brought it up with me in the room? I was wounded but curious about Chris's response.

"So, what did you say?"

"I told her there isn't much I can do. You make your own choices," he said.

A heavy silence filled the room. I tried to think of an excuse but had none. Instead, I was bathed in shame, a sticky substance that covered me and weighed me down even more.

I was expecting him to give me an ultimatum, to say something to force me to get on track, but none was forthcoming.

In the quiet, I thought about offering a solution, ticking off the possibilities, like flipping through a recipe box.

Juice fast. Not healthy.

Weight Watchers. Been there, done that.

Low-carb. I had just heard a story saying that this wasn't good for you.

I had nothing to offer.

"I'll try to do better," I said, and left the room.

For the next few days, while his parents were still around, there was tension in the house. I was mad. Only years later did I realize it was because Robin was calling me out. She was speaking her truth instead of letting me wallow in my weight. She cared.

Chris's mother—my children's grandmother—was approaching seventy and was more fit and flexible than I was. I wondered if she worried about having to parent our kids if I died. I wondered if she thought I couldn't keep up with them at my size.

Instead of being happy that someone cared about me, I sulked. I went to work but called my friend Jessica, a fellow serial dieter. "I'm so mad she would say that to you," my friend said, though Robin hadn't said it to me. I wanted to hear that I'd been wronged, even though I knew my mother-in-law was right. Maybe I needed a bit of a smackdown but didn't like that it needed a filter. Or maybe I just wished that my weight was a nonissue.

One day, as I drove Robin back from getting her car serviced, I was a bit huffy.

"I know you're concerned, but I'm trying. I didn't put on any weight when I was pregnant. I work out. I have a garden," I said.

"I just worry about the kids, you know?"

Suddenly, all my rationalizing wasn't enough and it never would be, for me or for her. I agreed. I *was* hurting my kids.

And maybe Chris, too. Gone were the days of our

courtship, when I made chili from fresh chilies that I roasted myself and, once, a lasagna Bolognese that took seven hours to prepare. *Seven hours.* Now, I was lucky to have seven minutes to come up with dinner and, it seemed, even less time to make conversation with my husband.

After nearly a decade of marriage, I worried that we didn't see each other enough to talk about anything of consequence, even though we shared the same bed. Once, when an overweight family friend who struggled with diabetes and a host of other ailments was visiting with her husband, we watched him fetch her this and that, from a tissue to blow her nose to a piece of pie. Chris said to me, "That better not be you in a few years. You have to take care of yourself so I don't have to take care of you." I sat in our bed, shocked, and almost sniveling. *Wait, isn't that the point of marriage? To take care of each other?* His words cut through me, slicing a gully in my gut, straight through the layers of fat to the throbbing organs beneath.

Would it be the same if he were injured while running? He had run in seven marathons. More than once he felt a tugging in his chest. His doctor told him to take fish oil, but the giant jug of it sat on our shelf, barely touched. Or what if tongue cancer snuck up on him from the times he used chewing tobacco in college? Would I be off the hook? Would I want to be?

Of course not.

Chris rarely spoke of my weight. He shied away from the subject. When he did dare refer to my extra pounds, he was often met with my animosity. I was the elephant in the room. My weight was the thing that couldn't be discussed, and when it was, there was hell to pay.

My parents' marriage lasted fourteen years, though it was over after a decade, when my father started to wander, to cheat, while my mother was home taking care of us. As Chris and I approached our ten-year anniversary, I wondered if our marriage had a similar expiration date.

Every time my husband went out, I worried that was it. That was the end. He'd meet someone else, someone thinner, and leave me.

Yet when he came home and wanted to have sex, I often refused him. It usually was the first moments after I'd finally had a shower, washed off the stink of being a three-hundred-pound woman, and felt fresh again.

One night, after I rolled my eyes when Chris made a move, he snapped.

"This isn't some kind of chore, Kara."

But it was. Everyone and everything was pulling at me, asking me for something. Emily needed to nurse. Anna needed affection. Chris did, too. But I felt like, despite my enormity, my overabundance of flesh, I had nothing left to give. I just wanted a moment to myself, even though I hated myself.

I wondered if I was carving out my own divorce decree. Writing it ahead of time as if it was destiny. I didn't feel worthy of marriage.

I was still scarred from the fights between my parents. My mother would scream into the telephone receiver when my father was out with another woman, then hand the phone to me. "Tell your father to come home," she'd say.

"Put your mother back on the phone," he'd demand.

I heard the phone click and then the dial tone that held the air and then my mother sobbing into her pillow.

"I'm so sorry, sweetheart," she'd say.

Even now, my fears of that time, of that moment, of that lonely dial tone remain.

Every time Chris was late or opted to go out with his running group, I wondered if he'd find a fitter partner for his life.

And why shouldn't he? How could anyone love me, broken with food and a bound-up mess of worry and sorrow? My solution was to not talk about it, to not make it his problem. I kept quiet and dealt with everything in my head but solved nothing.

It didn't help that Chris had always earned more than I did and sometimes seemed to resent that my salary needed to be supplemented. This created a dynamic where I was afraid to ask for anything, whether money or time—to take a walk or go out. I felt unworthy or that it wouldn't be worth it to ask. As a result, I had debts Chris didn't know about. I'd smile when creditors called my phone and pretend they were telemarketers.

I also resented playing second fiddle to his marathon goals, which required months of training and gobbled our weekends with his miles and then his recovery. I just wanted to get outside, though it was easy enough for me to miss a workout, then another, then suddenly, my big body made it feel like I was starting from scratch, a rookie at the gym. I kept my voice soft, muted my demands, but I had needs. Lots of them.

Especially as my body grew beyond my frame.

We were headed to Lake Tahoe for Chris's cousin's wedding, which happened to fall on my birthday. We bought three airline seats, one for me, one for Anna, and one for Chris. Emily and my extra girth would have to fit somewhere in that tight row. A squeeze, but doable because Anna was still small and occupied only half a seat.

Emily mostly sat on my lap. Anna jockeyed into position, trying to smoosh me over. It was the first time we'd flown together that she tried to own her own space. I was mortified that she might call out something like, "Move over, Mom, you're in my seat."

But she didn't. People who saw me on the plane gave me that same frightened "Please don't be seated next to me" look. They needn't have worried. I was only going to squish my own family.

I had to remind Chris to lift his armrest, which he did without complaint other than a little roll of his eyes. Then the seatbelt extension came. I thought I wouldn't need one as I pulled and tugged at the strap, making sure it wasn't caught under the seat. I was pretty close to having it fit, but it didn't, not quite. I was sure if I could nudge a little more to the right, I could get the metal tab to click in. But I wouldn't have room to breathe, let alone manage the constant entertainment of two young girls on a plane, including fetching snacks and coloring books from backpacks and making quick changes in the rest room after accidents with flying apple juice.

No. I needed the seatbelt extender. The flight attendant was discreet, thank goodness.

Finally, we settled in. Chris read, and Emily gnawed on her *Very Hungry Caterpillar* book, about a creature that could never get enough, that ate more and more every day—first fruits, then chocolate cake, then pickles, then ice cream, then Swiss cheese. That poor binging caterpillar didn't feel better until he ate a leaf. Hand it to greens to save the day.

To most parents, it's a counting book, something to help their kids learn the days of the week, colors, and numbers. For me, it was personal. I just hoped the flight attendant wouldn't see it.

When we landed, the trip started with a highlight—a

reunion with my high school friend Julia. She had been the best tennis player in the state. Though big in a Game-of-Thrones-Brienne way, she'd never been fat. But when I saw her, it took an extra moment for my eyes to process her transformation. The two of us matched, a pair of three-hundred-pounders.

I was aghast to see her that way. Hadn't she seen how unhappy I was, how much I struggled? Wasn't that motivation enough to take care of herself? I didn't know how to talk about it, to make light of the fact that we were both huge. So we didn't. We just caught up over a glass of wine, talking about our friends from high school and how they were all just the same as life went along. Except us, both of us bigger, out of breath while walking up the stairs in ill-fitting clothes.

I knew how hard it was to go anywhere else, once you were there, to get rid of that size that has settled on your bones.

Julia was there.

The next morning, as we said goodbye, Chris took a photo. In it, our bodies were nearly identical, our faces were just as big as each other's. We also took a photo of our daughters together. I worried about all of us. How did we do this to ourselves? Were we doing the same thing to our kids?

With Chris at the wheel driving us to Yosemite, on our way to Tahoe, I looked at the photos, flipping back and

forth between them, trying not to get car sick on the wind-
ing, redwood-lined roads.

"It was hard seeing Julia that way," I said.

There was silence. The kids were sleeping in the back.
Wind whistled through the trees along the roadside. He
asked, "Do you think it was hard for her to see you that
way?"

"I've always been this way."

As soon as I said them, I wanted to eat my words. I
hated seeing Julia that way. When would I hate seeing myself this way?

I wondered if my pattern of eating was not only sliding
down onto my family but also onto my friends. Did Julia
think it was okay to be heavy because I was? What could I
do to break this pattern?

I was relieved when we finally reached the restaurant
where we were meeting our family and the wedding party.
The place was cozy, and we could see Chris's other cousins
and aunts and uncles gathered beneath the canopy toward
the back. I had to scoot my way through the restaurant,
past tables and chairs, with my huge hips and butt at the
level of everyone's meal, while toting an excited child and
unwieldy baby and all their gear.

"Excuse me," I said to the first person who tried to
move in when she saw me coming. My body squeezed and
then expanded as it passed between chair backs in the over-
crowded venue.

"Oops. Just going to squish through here," I said to the next person, with a fake smile, and the next. People automatically moved when they saw me coming.

I bet they wondered, "Wonder what she's been eating?"

I hadn't seen this side of the family in months, some since I'd lost the 120 pounds and climbed Kilimanjaro for the first time. I was nearly at my heaviest, and though I tried to come up with a few stories about how I was getting back into fitness, or all the walking we did in Yosemite, I could tell that all they saw was *fat*. Chris's fat wife. Chris's inspiring but crazy fat wife.

There were lots of hugs, where I could feel fingers pressing into my flab, as if to gauge my real size. I knew there was love, but I usually avoided hugging so others couldn't feel the solidity of my flesh.

It was hard to feel good about any part of my looks, though I'd bought some new clothes for this trip—billowy, fresh clothes that were big but that (unsuccessfully) hid my body with A-line shapes and such. I self-consciously pulled my new shirt, bedazzled with rhinestones, down over my new pants, making sure that no seams had split. That I didn't have baby food smeared all over my shoulder. Wasn't I enough of a spectacle already?

The next day we all took a hike to Emerald Bay State Park, a five-hundred-foot drop via glacier-carved granite that led to Vikingsholm, a Scandinavian architectural lake cottage.

I carried seven-month-old Emily in the Ergo carrier, huffing and sweating. Chris's parents were with us, and he and his dad, Jim, were high-tailing it up ahead, like the runners they were. I worried they were talking about how slow I was, as my feet slid on the gravel path. I was afraid I would fall and crash on top of our daughter, crushing her. I stopped and pretended to admire the waterfalls or the roots that jutted out like trees themselves, but I was just catching my breath.

My mother-in-law, thoughtful as always, waited for me.

"Can't believe—they walked—ahead," I said, panting. "Left us carrying the baby." Robin asked to have a turn. "No. I've got it," I said. I could feel my chest moving up and down as Emily slept, but I didn't want to disturb her. Perhaps because I had carried Emily in my belly, it seemed obvious that I should continue carrying her wherever we went. But walking uphill, carrying my own pounds and her nearly twenty pounds, exhausted me. Sweat matted my hair, soaked the edges of the baby carrier, and dripped down my back in an uncomfortable tickle.

Anna sprinted ahead to try to beat Chris and Jim, and, suddenly, my heart lifted. I watched her dig her toes into the path and pump her arms, then I took a deep breath and tried to finish strong with her. I didn't run, but I got to see her flash past Jim and Chris, dust kicking up from her shoes.

Maybe I was being left behind, but Anna wasn't. There was solace in that.

That night we gathered for the rehearsal dinner, an early evening picnic in a grove of sequoias that reached to the heavens and took us along with them. I perched on a camp bench (fearing the folding chairs would collapse under my weight) and surveyed the spread: barbeque burgers, ribs, and hot dogs atop red-checkered tablecloths—the most beautiful picnic I'd ever seen, with the sounds of the forest in the background and the children running into the woods to play.

I was glad to give up my giggling baby to others and catch up with the adults, particularly Troy, my husband's cousin, who had just had a heart attack. He glommed on to me like a gnat, seemingly determined to talk me into being healthier. "I got rid of all carbs, and the weight just dropped," he confided.

Of course, I thought. *I'll start doing that too.*

He was wearing new clothes, since his sixty-pound weight loss, and it may have been the first time I saw him tuck in his shirt instead of letting it, along with his belly, hang over his belt. I had to admit that he looked great, but I was jealous, too. My mind rifled through all the reasons he was more vulnerable to a heart attack than I was. He was a smoker. He had high blood pressure. His blood sugar had been off the charts.

I, on the other hand, had perfect numbers, other than the one on the scale. Then again, my father had his first heart attack at thirty-one. Would my bad habits catch up with me, like they did with Troy? I saw him head toward the woods with a cigarette in his hand and his wife, also puffing away. Over the years, she'd also dropped forty pounds. Though smoking certainly wasn't a solution for me.

I didn't really want to hear about Troy's weight loss. I wanted to enjoy my food and my family. Anna was playing off in the distance with her cousins. I could hear their laughter as they found hiding spots among the trees. Emily was happy in someone else's arms. I looked up at the sky and appreciated the moment, the kids all cared for, and thought, for once, about how lucky I was. How very blessed for the little things and a chance to just breathe.

With no children tugging on me, I could eat a meal of burgers and coleslaw like an adult instead of sneaking bits into my mouth and feeling unsatisfied in the end. I savored every bite, inhaling the scent of the forest all around and sipping a microbrew. It was all too perfect, with the sun arching down the trunks of the towering sequoias. Then I noticed that I couldn't see Anna. I remembered there were bears in these woods, and I panicked, certain that she had been dragged away and was being mauled. I stood and turned in a circle so fast my vision blurred. What was she wearing? I couldn't remember. I could see other kids run-ning, but she wasn't with them.

"Anna? Anna!"

Suddenly, I spotted her, jumping up and down with ex-citement in the cedar-shingle garage, surrounded by a soft glow of candles. By her side were Chris and Robin with two huge cakes—one chocolate, one vanilla. Then the whole group turned toward me and erupted in "Happy Birthday."

It was my first surprise party. The sweetest birthday I ever had.

I was to have lunch with my former boss Caryn, who also struggled with her weight. We hadn't seen each other in a while, and she was anxious to get together. We'd agreed to meet at Marigold's, my favorite place in town, to get soup and salad, a healthy lunch. As she walked down the street, I recognized her smile—but not her body.

She was *thin,* which made me enormously jealous. I learned that she'd had gastric bypass surgery and lost more than a hundred pounds. I watched as she took a few spoonfuls of soup, a forkful or two of salad, and packed the rest to go. Our conversation was a blur.

All I could think was, *She's wasting away. She must be miserable. I could never be full with so little food. That would never work for me.*

I knew other people who'd had the surgery and who were dropping pounds like maple trees drop leaves in October. And there I was, holding steady at three hundred pounds, just as I had for most of the last two decades since college and twenty-five-cent draft nights.

I desperately wanted to call my Weight Watchers friend Jessica. At one time, we had bonded over low-fat muffins and lattes at Starbucks after our weekly weigh-ins, but now she lived in New Hampshire and I missed her. Hovering above two hundred pounds, she was one of the few people I could really talk to about my issues with food. We both wanted to get back in control, back to the days when we were Weight Watchers champions. "My sister just lost fifty pounds using this app that tracks your food," she'd tell me. "I've been using that and it's somewhat helpful."

Like anything, I was willing to give it a try.

Like the desk cycle, that sat under my desk unused.

Like the treadmill, still in my garage.

Like the rowing machine that I *had* to buy but hadn't unfolded for weeks. I knew exactly what I wanted to ask Jessica: *Was I crazy for not considering weight loss surgery?*

Food and fat covered up so much of what I was feeling: the embarrassment, the shame. The fact that I was even pausing to ask myself this question was significant. You might even say I was admitting that I had a problem and entertaining one way to solve it. Usually, when I went down this path my brain would get so intertwined with thoughts of what to have for breakfast, lunch, or dinner that I would forget the idea of eating healthier or any other action that would solve my dilemma.

It's not that I was unaware of my problem with food—that once I started eating, I couldn't stop, or that I used food to distract me from the unhappy details of my life. I wore my problem every day, carrying it around for everyone else to see.

For years, I'd blamed external factors. After all, food isn't like alcohol, where if you have a problem you can quit cold turkey. Food would always be a part of my life. I was like a cocaine addict forced to hang out in a crackhouse every night. Especially with the kids, there were so many snacks and little carby things that were part of my day, part of our culture. Goldfish, cookies, ice cream for any kind of celebration or snack. Sure, I could make one of those fancy faux sushi rollups often featured on the covers of healthy cookbooks, but who the hell had time for that?

I told myself I didn't. I could barely keep track of which days Anna liked cheese sticks and which days she didn't.

But I was getting to the point where I didn't want to blame anyone anymore. All I knew: dieting inevitably made me fatter.

So, what about weight loss surgery? Why didn't it seem like a simple decision? Especially when I'd seen family and friends spring into their new bodies so confidently, accomplishing in mere weeks what took others months and years to achieve, weight-loss-wise.

Jessica knew exactly why I was struggling. Someone in her office had just had the procedure. "It's totally messing with my head," she said.

As a heavy person, I was tremendously affected when others lost weight. My confidence plummeted, and their success underscored the fact that it might be possible for me to do something. But I was never sure I was ready for weight loss surgery. A distant relative ended up in a two-month coma after the surgery, and he still struggled with the effects of the brain injury. A colleague's husband died from an infection after the procedure. One of Jessica's relatives had the surgery but was fatter after than before.

Still, I knew people who said things like, "My only regret is that I didn't have it sooner."

And yet I wasn't ready. I told myself that it was expensive and we didn't have much money to spare. I told myself that we might want to have another kid—at thirty-nine, I didn't have much time left for that, and having the surgery would delay that option. In some ways, having surgery also felt like giving up, though it occurred to me that maybe *not* getting it was giving up. I had to worry about being around for my daughters. Did I have more of a chance of survival with the surgery or without it?

◇◇◇

That summer, we visited Chris's family's farm in Indiana. It was fun to be there, but not always easy or comfortable. For one thing, the full-size bed in Chris's room was more suited to a teenager. Every time we moved, the box spring tilted, making me worry it would collapse. The mattress was just as old, pancake thin, and I took up most of the bed.

We headed there shortly after our Lake Tahoe trip. The farmhouse was a gathering point for generations of my husband's family, with dark wood and built-in book shelves, hanging baskets of ferns, and a white porch dotted with overstuffed wicker chairs. The parlor had a piano and a round wooden table suitable for puzzles, board games, and conversation. The sprawling kitchen included a special low counter for rolling pie dough. There was a time when Jim's grandmother made a pie for each of the farmhands for lunch. They worked that hard and were that hungry.

I decided I needed to learn to be a little more like the Whitelys. Learn how to love. Learn how to be still and present instead of defensive. Learn how to eat from them. And let them teach my daughters.

They knew how to have fun with board games and puzzles and corn hole because they knew how to spend time with each other. Family life didn't need to be chaotic or uncomfortable, I realized. My own family was so fractured. I'd only met my mother's brothers and sisters and cousins in California a few times in my life.

At the farm, there was time for everyone, time to wait for homemade ice cream and pies to be ready while enjoying conversation and then enjoying the sweets together rather than eating in secret, as I so often did.

Chris's family is Quaker, so maybe that's why they all seemed so calm, thoughtful, and, most of all, peaceful. They have restraint; they can keep red and green Christmas M&Ms stored in the cabinets until the actual holiday and months after rather than eating them ahead of time and replacing them secretly in case someone was keeping candy inventory.

The fact that they all seemed to have it so together intimidated me. It wasn't until this August trip to the farm, where my in-laws spent their summers, that I really understood, despite nearly ten years of marriage to their son. On the family homestead, the night sky flickered with fireflies that danced above the grass and into the rows of corn. There was a magical stillness that we all felt, especially the girls, as they sat on the side porch, bathed and bellies full, and watched the nature show. Early in the evenings, we'd gather at the kitchen table to pinch the ends off green beans and toss them in enamel bowls or to talk about gardening and our struggles with the striped cucumber beetle.

We were on common ground.

Our visit turned out to be a special time for all of us. Calm and safe. I didn't want to leave, but school was starting soon and we had to head home. Anna was starting first grade at a new school. That meant shopping for shoes, paper, and pencils and establishing a new routine. And learning a new set of rules.

At Back-to-School night, parents gathered in our children's classroom at their miniature desks, and the teacher reviewed the curriculum and her expectations of the students. Then the nurse went over the "no sweets in the classroom" rule—not even for birthday celebrations.

She seemed to focus her gaze on me as she explained this policy. But maybe I was imagining it.

Anna's birthday arrived in February. Fresh off a snow day, she selected a book for me to read to her class about the science of snowflakes. Anna loved reading above anything. Her eyes were fixed on the classroom door and she spotted me the moment I arrived. She rose from her desk and ran to me. My cheeks blushed when I saw her; I was excited to see her in her element.

I was also overheated. I had agonized over what to wear that day, finally going with a black sweater and knit pants and a bright purple scarf around my shoulders to distract from the width of my hips, which were at eye level to the students.

But they would know. I held Anna in front of me as she guided me to the special reading chair, trying to steer her on a path around the periphery of the room that was the least visible to the gazes of her curious classmates, but

Anna paraded me right through the middle of everyone. I was her mom. I was there.

And I wanted to be there for her. My mother almost never showed up at school or sports events when I was growing up, and though it may have been because of her work schedule, I always thought she didn't care.

I wanted to show up. I wanted to be there for my girl, to celebrate her on any possible occasion. Yet I wanted to hide at the same time.

I lowered myself into the reading chair, thankfully a wide-ish rocking chair instead of a child-sized piece of furniture I surely would have broken. Anna sat on my lap, making me worry that my weight plus hers would be too much for the rocker, so I kept my feet firmly planted, thighs tensed. It was uncomfortable, but I was glad she was there to hide me.

Anna was intensely smart but painfully shy, often opting to stay in the classroom instead of navigating the playground at recess. She never knew how to penetrate a group to ask to play. I wondered if that was my fault, from not playing with her enough. I worried she would be unpopular, like I was.

To help her fit in, I worked hard to pick out clothes and shoes that other kids would like, such as shoes that blinked every time she walked. Shirts that made her sassy and cute, such as one that said "Smart Is the New Pretty."

She could fit into normal-sized clothes and I wanted her to fit in because I never did. Anytime I had tried to put on a normal-sized piece of clothing as a kid, I couldn't button it. My belly would stick out.

But Anna always looked perfect, but was especially so on her birthday. My eyes glistened with pride as she read. She grabbed my hand and begged to come home with me. Instead, I insisted she say because she had more things to learn.

At pickup time later that day, I couldn't wait to see her and hear how she had enjoyed the rest of her birthday. I beamed a smile as I spotted her coming through the door.

"Hey, Birthday Girl," I said, as she appeared.

Instead of a hug, she gave me a side glance and, without even a "Hello," she socked her turquoise-colored backpack into my gut. One of the things I was not prepared for as a parent was being used as a punching bag or any of the other seriously hurtful things that kids do to take out their feelings on their parents. I glanced around to see if any of the other parents had noticed Anna's gesture, and felt painfully embarrassed.

"What happened?" I asked, holding her bag in one hand, my stomach in the other.

She grunted.

"What happened?" I asked again, but gave her some

leeway as she sank down in the back of our messy Honda
Civic. It was her birthday after all.

"I hate Jenny," she said finally.

"Okay, what did Jenny do?" I asked.

"I don't want to tell you," Anna said. "She's just a jerk."

"Okay, well, when you want to talk about it, I'm here
for you," I said.

Jenny was a cute girl, with hair neatly pulled back in
gingham headbands and color-coordinated clothing. Jenny's family's house was amazing, with a pool and adjacent
organic garden. Her mother was thin and fit—an aromatherapist in training—and Anna admired everything about
their life, especially after Jenny's birthday party when she
and every guest received a stuffed animal.

But on Anna's birthday, after I'd left the classroom, the
teacher stepped out of the room for a moment and Jenny
had turned to Anna and blurted out, "Why is your mom
so fat?"

The whole class had laughed. Anna later told me she
said nothing. But she thought, "Don't talk about my mom
that way."

After that, she didn't talk to Jenny again. But I could
tell that she carried the worry that this kind of humiliation
could or would happen again. I was the main source of her
embarrassment, my fat making her a target. I was a glaring
example that something was off in her world.

I couldn't stand the thought of her carrying more in her life than she had to. I wanted to be there for her in her class, in her life—but when would me showing up become too embarrassing? She had already asked me to stop singing alongside her as we approached the school.

"Mom, cut it out," she would say, even though I was singing a Taylor Swift ditty that she loved in the privacy of our home.

How long before she refused to let me get out of the car during drop-off? How long before I couldn't get out of the car because it hurt too much or because I didn't want her friends to see me in my sloppy fat clothes, arm flab hanging out of my sleeveless dress, blue veins bubbling out of my legs?

When would it all be too much for her to take? For me to take?

I think it already was.

My dad had been sick for the last few weeks, and the night before, he'd gone into kidney failure. It didn't help that he had only one kidney after a tumor necessitated the removal of the other a decade earlier. I was considering visiting him.

Maybe it was anxiety, but I had developed a sharp pain in my right calf the evening before, after a few interviews for work. At first, I thought it was a muscle spasm. But it didn't go away. In fact, it got worse. As the smell of corned beef filled our condo—I was making a special meal for St. Patrick's Day—Chris and I agreed that I should go to the ER. Maybe it was a blood clot, a deep vein thrombosis, just like the ones my mother and father had had. The condition was hereditary, and I was at greater risk because of my weight. So I headed for the hospital, where the doctors did an ultrasound.

Luckily, the scan turned up nothing. But when I got home and climbed into bed, I couldn't get comfortable with the pain in my leg a constant source of tension. Finally, I got up and searched airfares for an affordable plane ticket to visit my father. I was worried I would need two seats when I couldn't pay for one. Even though Chris had assured me that if I felt I needed to see my father we would make it happen, I felt guilty. I was also angry. The fat that I'd gained after my father's departure from my life was keeping me from seeing him in what were possibly his final days.

Finally, I closed my computer. I'd made a decision. I couldn't afford two seats on an airplane. I could barely afford one. I would have to say goodbye to my father some other way.

I went back to bed, where I sobbed softly, pushing my face into Chris's sleeping body. His warmth consoled me, made me feel comforted and anchored. I cried for the man my father was and the man I wished he was. I'd worked hard to mend our relationship, but it wasn't ever a Hallmark bond. It never would be. The best I could do was to focus on my own children.

My father died the next day.

When my brothers and I met at his house a month later to sort through his things and prepare for the estate sale, I was surprised to see how proudly he displayed our photos—in frames in full view of his La-Z-Boy chair, where he spent most of his time—as if he had been with us throughout our childhoods. Maybe we had been a part of his life, even though we didn't know it. I was glad that he cared. But I still wished it had been different.

Front and center on his desk was a plaque that I had made for him in woodworking class in middle school. His name, *D. Richardson,* was stenciled in copper. I still remember the smell of the wood stain and how carefully I covered every inch of the wood with the dark hue. As I held the wooden sign, I recalled that this was the class where I had been bullied by two male classmates. Again, it was on my birthday, a year after I was sexually assaulted. The boys, who had heard about the police report, saw me walk in the room and yelled, "Sexual harassment, stop, drop, and roll!" They laughed and shouted until I ran from the room. As

I fled, I thought of my father. My father, the Navy Seal, could have wiped the floor with those punks if he had been around. But he wasn't. The other kids were bringing their plaques home to their dads. I had to ship mine.

Still, I liked the idea of my dad, even when he opted not to be in my life. Apparently, he liked the idea of being my dad, too. Upstairs, I noticed my first book, sitting neatly on top of a pile of magazines and periodicals where my stories had been featured. He rarely called, so I assumed he never thought of me, much less my career. But there I was, in his home.

My heart shattered into a million pieces, and I sobbed in the bathroom. My stomach quivered as I sat, surrounded by my father's things, trying to remember the good and let go of the bad. It was all I could do.

That quiver in my belly wasn't just grief. It was a son, conceived in the week of my father's death when I was so wrapped up in his illness that I forgot to take my birth control pills.

"Well, we may have a bit of a surprise," I told Chris.

I didn't really want to be pregnant and I didn't really not want to be pregnant. So I went to my doctor to be sure.

"Listen, if there isn't a heartbeat, it's okay. I don't feel pregnant," I told the obstetrician before the first ultrasound. "I've come to terms with the fact that there may not be anything going on in there."

The technician squeezed a bit of cold goop on my belly, and then, realizing the size of my abdomen, got another tube.

I'd already had a pee test confirm that I was pregnant, but other than those tiny bouts of queasiness, I didn't feel pregnant. I stopped taking the pill just in case I was.

As I felt the technician push the ultrasound wand against my billowy body, I braced myself for there to be a heartbeat. I braced myself for there not to be a heart-beat. There are so many cautions about plus-size pregnancies. Even though I'd never had a problem, I wondered if my body could handle this, bringing another child safely to term. I didn't believe my body could support more life.

The tech squinted and nodded, pursing her lips. This was supposed to be my six-week check, the moment when the tech discovers whether there is a heartbeat. She was looking for a shape no bigger than a lima bean.

As soon as she pressed the wand into my fat, I heard it. One hundred fifty-five beats per minute, the beautiful symphony I'd heard each time a doctor or ultrasound tech checked on my two daughters. A heart beating inside of me that was not my own. It belonged to my baby.

"When did you say your last period was?"

"Well, it's hard to tell. I don't remember. There's been a lot going on lately. . . ."

"Sweet pea, looks like there's a thirteen-week-old baby in there," she said. "And, well, do you want to know any-thing more about the little one?"

I could barely catch my breath from the sound of the fast-beating heart, knowing all at once that I was growing something so important inside of me.

"Yes, please. Anything?"

"I mean, do you want to know the gender?"

"Oh, yes, of course. I hate surprises—except this one," I said.

"It's still a little early, but I'd say there's a ninety-five percent chance it's a boy."

Oh boy.

◇◇◇

Elliott James Whitely came into this world a full pound heavier than his sisters had been—not the gigantic baby one doctor had predicted because of my size at the beginning of the pregnancy. Actually, I didn't gain any weight during this pregnancy. The doctor just worried the baby would be big because I was big.

Happy, healthy—and born, luckily, head down, after a little scare when he flipped the week of his birth.

Elliot was conceived the same week my father died, and he was born on my father-in-law's birthday. These two men, so disconnected, but each a piece of this child.

My father was a financial mess. My father-in-law is a responsible role model.

My father left his family. My father-in-law is passionate about preserving his.

My father forgot me, leaving a bottomless pit of abandonment. My father-in-law learned to love me despite first impressions. He made me a part of his life because I was a part of his son's.

I can't imagine a more beautiful and wondrous thing—to feel accepted. To feel loved. To accept those offerings even when we are afraid we don't deserve them.

My kids will never feel forgotten or unloved. And, just maybe, neither would I.

Life pressed ahead faster than expected. We were swept up in a whirlwind of moving to a home big enough for our family of five.

Anna was in second grade. Emily was in preschool. Elliott was a healthy, happy boy.

I was conflicted about my father's death. And yet the world kept turning.

I had been grieving ever since our family split. But, since dad's death, it was a kind of a relief not to keep being disappointed that he wasn't part of my life in the way I wanted or needed him to be. There wasn't that moment of anxiety, hoping he wouldn't forget to call me on my birthday even though it fell two days after his.

We moved when I was super-pregnant with Elliott, so a lot was left packed. Our new house looked like a mountain range of cardboard boxes. When I finally got around to unpacking, I made a rule that if I hadn't used something in seven years, I was getting rid of it.

Then I came upon a set of plates my father gave me.

They were the ones my parents had registered for when they got married. Some pieces had been chipped long ago, probably because I'd put them away too quickly when rushing through my childhood chores. They were Franciscan Earthenware, a Madeira pattern—brown and green dishes, covered in dust. When my father gave them to me years ago, I was overwhelmed by nostalgia and joy. But I didn't use them; I put them away up in the cabinet above the fridge. Like my father was during my childhood, they were out of reach.

Nearly a year after my father died, these dishes and some furniture were all I had left of him. I knew I would keep them. But instead of feeling warm and happy to hold them in my hands, they made me anxious. The plates, brown with a very seventies swirling-flower design, were white hot with memories. Memories of my father's empty place setting, memories of loading them with food to ease my sadness.

I kept the dishes, but they went in the garage in a box wedged between other relics of the histories of our lives.

Meanwhile, my life was full. I had Chris, the house, the baby, and my big girls. Anna was trying new things— soccer, basketball, and volleyball. She was becoming the girl I wished I could have been, with the childhood I wished I had had. I struggled to keep up with Emily, who was a comet of energy, always interested in things. Elliott was a giggly baby, who laughed at the slightest silly look.

Our family was complete. While over-the-moon grateful for our little surprise of a third child, Chris and I were absolutely sure we didn't want any more children. This decision was both freeing and mortifying. I was now in control of my body. I would never again be harnessed by an umbilical cord. My body was now mine and mine alone.

I still breastfed, but this time I let formula supplement what I couldn't provide. The pregnancy had taxed my body in ways I didn't expect, and, maybe because of my "advanced maternal age" of forty-one, it was harder than ever to bounce back. Maybe it was because I had to keep track of three beings. The late-night feedings left me harried, like a coffee-crazed air traffic controller. I spent my days in stretchy "active wear," the only clothes that felt comfortable because my weight was closer to 320 pounds months after Elliott's birth. I binged and grazed all day long, stuffing away my tiredness and frustration. When the girls fought over the remote control or I couldn't find Elliott's tiny shoe, I ate. When Emily took off her jacket moments after I succeeded in getting it onto her little wriggly body, I ate. When I was too tired to play games and read books, I ate.

My body grew bigger.

My heart grew heavier.

I looked at my sweet children and worried they would be left without a mother, the way I was without a father. My weight was dangerous, and I felt powerless to change it. But I knew I had to. I had spent the past eight years bringing these children into the world. Now I had to find myself so I could be their mom for as long as possible.

Part Two

*R*ain pelted down, splashing on the sidewalk as my friend Brigid and I sat in the window of Café Batavia. This downtown Summit teak-furniture-turned-coffee-shop featured the bright, sunny work of local artists and a flickering electric fireplace. Being seated in the window made me uncomfortable, as if I were on display like a sideshow act, with my thighs flapping over the sides of the wooden chair. *Would the chair hold?* I wondered, as I often did.

Still, I had needed to get out of the house. Everything in my body constantly hurt. I was a forty-two-year-old 330-pound mother of three kids.

It had come to this. After the birth of dear, sweet Elliott, I was more exhausted than I'd ever been. It took all appendages pushing with all their strength to roll my body from one side to the other, my belly flopping over too, a separate entity unto itself. The weight of my hips pressed down on the bone structure beneath and my legs skewed at inappropriate angles because my anatomy was so compromised.

Just standing was an effort. Every time I did it, I needed a moment to gather myself beforehand, to wonder if my legs would even work. Every time, I had to grab hold of a table, a chair, anything solid to help anchor myself as I hoisted my torso to a vertical position.

Strangers' stares had become more pointed. Though I had always loved the outdoors, I became a homebody. Chris tried to get me out on hikes, but I had only excuses, not enthusiasm.

I could see and feel his disappointment. Like he was losing me.

Each time I went to the toilet, the flow of urine splashed my rump, but my arms couldn't quite reach around to wipe. I accepted this, the humiliation of letting the urine dry on my skin because I couldn't clean it all off. Because of my gluttony, because of my food problem, it would be my fate to smell like urine all day long.

I focused more on whether I'd be able to get up from the toilet. Which part of me would creak, give out, or fuse to the seat, making it even harder to stand.

Inside, it felt as if my organs were suffocating under the weight of my flesh and that my limbs were coming apart. I walked when I had to. I did chores. I went through six hundred tablets of ibuprofen in a couple of months. And everything still hurt.

When I lay down, I pointed my toes and stretched my legs as long as I could, trying to relax them after they'd been compacted by the weight of me all day long. I longed for one of those medieval torture devices to stretch my spine back into its original shape.

Just *being* was exhausting. I was working from home and didn't have to get out of my pajamas. (A good thing, because I'd grown out of most plus sizes.) And because I was home, with little to distract me, all I thought about, from morning till night, was food and my weight.

So when Brigid asked me out to coffee so I could help her get into blogging, I accepted, though finding something to wear was near impossible. I opted for yoga pants and told myself, and her, that I would be working out later that day, which proved to be false.

We talked about the ins and outs of finding your voice, of sharing, and of oversharing. We talked about writing about weight, which I did a lot.

"There's something only three people know," she said. "I had weight loss surgery five years ago. I lost more than seventy pounds."

I found my eyes scanning her body, from her thick, curly blonde hair, down to her cute-fitting jeans tucked into Wellies (boots that would never have fit over my calves).

I hadn't known her as a fat person. We'd met two years prior, when our kids were in the same class. I'd always thought she had a body I would love to have—strong, not too skinny. She was someone who looked like a human being who ate and enjoyed food and life. And she had always been kind to me, especially because our kids were fond of each other. And it was clear that Brigid and I both loved to laugh as we navigated through life as parents of second graders.

She went on to explain that she had wanted the surgery so much that she paid for it out of pocket—$30,000, money saved for a new car. I knew she lived in a nicer house than I did, but that seemed like more money than I could ever dredge up, even for something as life-changing as surgery. "But that's only because insurance wouldn't cover it. Maybe your insurance would cover you."

I hadn't said anything about surgery. I thought maybe she was dropping a hint. In the past, this might have bothered me. But this time, out of the hundreds, if not thousands, of other hints and suggestions dropped near me, I wanted to listen.

"It was worth it. You might lose some hair, but that happens with most surgeries. It will grow back," she said. "I just wanted to be on a level playing field."

I totally knew what she meant. I was always the heaviest person at Weight Watchers meetings. When someone tried to sympathize, saying they wanted to drop twenty or even thirty pounds, I knew that I had to add a one in front of that number. They would be finishing just as I would be getting started.

Leveling the playing field was exciting to imagine. I always started behind the pack, whether it was hiking Mount Kilimanjaro or doing a 5K walk, which I finished last. Maybe I didn't need to be left behind forever.

I was curious and wanted to know everything. She told me what her kids had thought and her husband and detailed what she ate every day. She could eat just about anything, just less of it. She explained that the surgery involved cutting out about 85 percent of her stomach, and that she'd been in the hospital for two nights, though she could have left after one. She was back to working at home just days after the procedure, and back in the office within a few weeks. It was that easy.

"It was no big deal," she said. "Really. It was the best decision I ever made."

"Wow," I said. "Maybe I should think about it too."

Saying this surprised me. I didn't think I'd ever consider surgery seriously. Now, it seemed like the only thing I could do.

I told her I had more thinking to do. I'd just had a baby, so maybe it wasn't time yet. And . . . it was *surgery,* with all its attendant risk. But I asked her the name of her surgeon, just in case.

Later that day, back at home, I microwaved some popcorn and while it popped I searched my phone for her surgeon's number. Her words kept coming back to me: *"It was the best decision I ever made."*

Normally, my brain was occupied with looking for the next bite, something to snack on without Chris or my kids knowing, but now, for the first time in a long time, I felt this glimmer of hope.

It was the best decision I ever made.

Maybe it could be mine, too.

I don't know why this time seemed different from when my cousin, my boss, and my friend had opted for surgery. Maybe it wasn't. Maybe it was because I hadn't known that Brigid had done it and she seemed like such a normal person. Maybe I was just ready to hear her message.

I went to my computer, looked up her surgeon, and called his office. Within minutes, I learned that they didn't take my insurance. I quietly pouted for a moment. Then, I was relieved. I mean, surgery was drastic, wasn't it? I could die.

But I wasn't really living, anyway. The profoundness of this nearly crushed the ceiling and walls in around me. The structure, the excuses, everything that held me hostage to *this is the way I am* started to crumble. I decided to make another phone call.

My husband's company had this service called Accolade, which provided a health care advocate. After one phone call, they connected me with a nurse and found Dr. Ragui Sadek of Advanced Surgical & Bariatrics, a surgeon who was covered because his office was a Blue Center of Excellence, meaning that he adhered to strict practices and had a certain success rate so that Blue Cross Blue Shield could send patients there.

"I'm still not sure if I want to do this," I said.

The nurse answered sweetly, "That's okay. You have the information if you want to move forward."

There was a way for me to do this. I was covered. I had often used lack of money as an excuse for not doing things, for not joining a gym or not hiring a personal trainer. Now I couldn't do that.

I called my friend Julia in California. In the years since I saw her during my California trip, she had had the surgery.

"It's the best decision I ever made," she said. Those magic words again. "I'm so glad you're asking me about it. You can ask me anything."

And I did. I pelted her with questions about how much extra skin she had (not much) and what her energy level was (higher than it had been in years). I wanted to make sure she could still eat the things I loved. I wanted everything to be the same—coffee, ice cream, alcohol, meat—but different.

Then I went online looking for information to assuage my doubts and fears about the surgery.

There were a few methods of weight loss surgery. There was the band, where a device was wrapped around the stomach to create a physical barrier, an impediment to eating too much.

There was gastric bypass, which involved creating a pouch of the stomach and rerouting the intestines to restrict the kinds of foods a person could eat.

And there was the gastric sleeve, which seemed like the best option for me. They would pump my abdomen full of air to create room for the surgeon and team to insert tools at five points near my belly and slice away at this vital organ, reducing its size by 85 percent.

I couldn't get enough of the details. For years, I had been horrified at the idea of surgery, at taking that kind of risk, when I should simply summon up the willpower and lose the weight myself. But I couldn't summon up the willpower; hadn't for two decades. And now, Julia, who had given birth via two C-sections, said the recovery was a walk in the park.

"I would have this surgery again and again," she told me. She was prone to a bit of exaggeration. She was the kind of person who put as many exclamation points as would fit in every note. I knew she was telling the truth, but to my ears it sounded like a little too much enthusiasm. I had to be careful.

Weight loss surgery was not a new idea for me. Decades ago, I'd read that it was the best solution for people who were morbidly obese. At the time, I didn't want to believe it. I was even a bit scornful. I'd just lost 120 pounds. How could someone be so incredibly stuck with their weight that there was *no other option* than to slice open their guts and permanently alter their stomach, the seat of nourishment? I wondered how desperate a person would have to be—how desperate I'd have to be—to make that choice.

Now I knew, because I was there. Unable to move in a way that gave me joy. Constantly uncomfortable.

I'd used up all my other options and I was mad that I ever judged anyone for making the decision to get surgery.

People had always said, "Make sure you get the weight off before you turn forty, because after that, it's impossible."

Of course I will, I had thought. Of course I didn't. I was now forty-two.

That admonition went the way of all others my elders gave me when I was in my twenties: wear sunscreen; make the most of your time before you have kids and a career; save your pennies.

I did none of those things, as if time was not a factor for me. And now, here I was, halfway through the average adult life span. Like I was gazing from the peak of a mountain, I could clearly see my path to the bottom, and I didn't want to bring along all the extra baggage I'd carried to the top. I didn't want to heft around the extra pounds anymore, to act like an eighty-year-old each time I got to my feet. If I hurt so much now, it seemed inevitable that

I'd lose all mobility at some point. I'd climbed mountains. Now I was headed for a cane, a walker, a wheelchair.

This was my moment to gain control, to claim a stake in my future and the future of my body. I knew it would be good for my family too—so I could be an active mom. So I could be a wife for life, and not drop dead of obesity complications.

Now, I just needed to convince Chris that this was a good idea.

The idea of talking to Chris about weight loss surgery frightened me. Even though he lived in the same house with me, and knew I struggled with food, he just didn't get it. Mostly that was because of me, not him. I hid my struggle—stuffing any snack food wrappers deep down in the garbage, locked in shame and embarrassment over the fact that food held such power over me. That night, after I got the kids to sleep, I went downstairs with one hand on the wall and one on the railing, trying to cushion the impact of my weight on my knees, and slumped next to Chris.

"So, guess who had weight loss surgery?"

Before he could answer, I announced, "Brigid. I never would have guessed. She can eat pretty normally now and she's doing great. I can't stop thinking about what she told me. She said it was the best decision she ever made, which is the same thing Julia told me. So the question is, why am I not making that decision?"

"What decision? Weight loss surgery? That's a terrible idea," Chris said.

"Why?"

"Because it's surgery. That can't be good for you." He got up to refill his water glass. "You've lost weight before. You can do it again."

He may not have noticed that I was too fat to wear my wedding ring. I had taken it off a week earlier when I noticed a purple lump had formed on my ring finger that pulsated and ached, like every other part of me. I knew at once that it was a blood vessel about to burst. My finger was tender to touch, but I touched it anyway, knowing that I needed to remove my wedding rings as soon as possible or my fingers would swell around them, and I would have to cut the bands.

I hadn't realized how my fingers had grown around my rings over the years. How there was a space that light and air did not touch. How my fat crept around my wedding rings, trapping fluid, tissue, and blood above it to the point that my blood vessels could no longer take it.

When I took off my ring, my finger almost sighed with relief. I could feel the fluid and blood trickling down to refill the pouched-in part of my finger where my ring had been. My skin was so indented, it looked like I was wearing a ring when I was not.

I hadn't taken off my engagement ring since the day

Chris put it on my finger. I'm not sure how he did it, but he had sized it perfectly, in secret, and kept it hidden until he asked me to marry him on the fourth anniversary of the day we started dating.

That diamond was purchased by a graduate student who was very good with money. In other words, it was easy to see, but not one of those blinding rocks that twinkle even in the shade.

I loved it. The ring—a simple solitaire on a white gold band—fit my finger and my personality. It also fit our love: not too showy but very sincere. It had always fit.

Until now.

That felt sad, especially because I didn't have a choice in the matter. Some people swell up when they're pregnant, but that didn't happen with me. I'd never had to remove my rings. But here I was, not pregnant, just fat, and without wedding rings because if I kept them on, I'd lose a finger, the rings, or both.

"I guess you're right," I said to Chris and got up.

I didn't know what else to say.

Chris had gone along with every weight loss idea I'd ever had. When I got rid of the "white stuff," he went along with my bread-, rice-, and potato-free life. He climbed Kilimanjaro with me. When I wanted to walk a half marathon, he ran the full length of it and we finished at the same time. He and his father lugged my NordicTrack rowing machine up two flights of stairs just so I'd have a place to work out in my office if there was no way to get to the gym. But I couldn't remember the last time I used it.

I had all the tools I needed to start dropping pounds. But somehow, all those tools, all my knowledge, amounted to nothing. I couldn't get going. I couldn't find a path to a healthy way of eating. Surgery was the only option I had left. But Chris's negativity gave me pause. Maybe it was a terrible idea. Maybe I would die.

But wasn't I already dying? I sure as hell wasn't living.

The sheaf of pre-appointment paperwork rivaled in thickness some of the diet books in my house. I had to fill out every weight-related ailment and family history fact so the experts at Advanced Surgery & Bariatrics in Somerset, New Jersey, could determine whether weight loss surgery was a good option for me. I wanted to be a model patient, one of the after pictures they posted on their website.

I passed quickly through the ailments: no diabetes, no heartburn (except a bit when I was pregnant), no high cholesterol.

Then I came to the joint pain part:

My pen dug deep into the page to check yes to every option—pain, burning, stiffness, popping in my knee. Pain, at times, in my hip. Pain in my back (though I didn't check that off because I assumed it resulted from me contorting myself like a Cirque de Soleil performer when nursing Elliott at night).

For years, I'd rationalized my weight with the fact that, despite the high number on the scale, my other numbers—blood pressure, cholesterol, and blood sugar—were all normal. Perfect, even.

Now, my body was telling a different story, even if I hadn't quite caught up.

Some answers I didn't fill in, such as the two places on the form to note my weight. Not because I didn't know but because I didn't want to believe that I was somewhere in the neighborhood of 330 pounds, nearing my peak weight of 360 pounds.

Sometimes Anna asked how much I weighed and I didn't want to tell her. I didn't want to admit how much I'd grown sideways.

Even Emily, only three, was noticing.

"I don't like your big butt. I like my small butt. Get rid of your big butt," Emily said. I started to worry that she was obsessing about my weight, but then her hands would move down to my feet.

"I don't like your big feet. I like my little feet," she'd say.

"Well, sweetie, those aren't changing. Those will always be there, and my feet have been very good to me."

◇◇◇

Somerset was a town on the border of Middlesex County, and the doctor's office was along an industrial drive of office buildings, many with medical testing boxes sitting outside their doors. Not bothering to look for the staircase, I took the elevator to the second floor and entered Dr. Sadek's office to hear the receptionist saying, "Okay, hope you feel better" to a patient on the phone.

I immediately assumed there were complications from a previous procedure. I wondered exactly what those might be and whether I would experience the same thing.

Why was I even here?

Ironically, the waiting room TV blared a talk show with a plus-size bride as guest. I cringed thinking that that was how I looked on my wedding day. Even though I was smiling and joyful in my photos, holding a russet rose bouquet I made with Japanese maple leaves around it, no amount of makeup, no amount of tulle could hide my size.

The receptionist handed me a brochure featuring a photo of innards. There was a stomach, glossy and pink, a pear-shaped organ linking the esophagus to an equally glossy small intestine. This was where digestion occurred.

I wondered what I looked like inside. How mangled and distorted had I made my guts? For years, I had stuffed them beyond capacity. Now I was planning to slaughter them.

The materials explained that the sleeve procedure would leave me with a banana-shaped pouch—with just enough room for a half cup of food.

"The first step of the rest of your life starts here," the brochure said.

The waiting room was getting crowded, though only three (big) patients were there, people, like me, who filled the sturdy, extra-wide chairs (almost benches) to capacity. I shifted on my bench when my name was called to go in to talk with Dr. Melman, Dr. Sadek's associate.

She seemed so precise, with her hair tucked back in a neat bun and tiny glasses. She showed me a video about how the stomach would be decreased to the shape of a four-ounce banana, leaving just a pouch for the food to come in. She explained that surgery would decrease a hormone called ghrelin, which was responsible for making me think I was hungry even when I wasn't. It was one of the mysteries of obesity—why certain people couldn't seem to get to the off switch when eating. That feeling of boundless hunger and emptiness, she promised, would be gone.

On the way home, I went a mile out of my way to find a drive-through McDonald's to order a milkshake. When the guy asked me if I wanted whipped cream and a cherry on top, I said yes. I didn't know how much more whipped cream and cherries would be in my life. Even though it didn't taste very good, I slurped it down, making sure I finished before I got home. My brain buzzed from the sugar overload.

I decided to meet with my former newspaper boss, Caryn, again. When we'd met for lunch more than a year earlier, she took most of her meal to go. I hadn't recognized her; I thought she looked emaciated. But then again, I'd only known her as fat.

This time, as I sat with her at Starbucks, I thought she looked amazing. I, on the other hand, was a mess, in a black, shapeless dress, with unshaven legs and only half a pedicure—Emily must have been doing something dangerous as I removed the enamel, causing me to stop midtask. The story of my life.

My skin was pasty, so I wore my dress with pants, hoping it would look like a long tunic. Instead, it looked like a dress with pants. As I gazed at myself in the mirror, dissatisfied, I set my phone down, then tore through the laundry basket, trying to find socks, until the pile of clothes covered the phone and I had to search for it.

"I'm the definition of a hot mess today," I told her. My heart was still pounding from lugging the car seat inside. Elliott's green eyes beamed up.

"Sorry, I thought he'd be sleeping. He needs a nap. So do I," I said.

"No, no worries," she said. "I'm just glad to get a chance to meet the little guy."

There was a joy in her that I had never seen before; it wasn't just her weight. I was happy for her, but also jealous.

Actually, I had noticed it months before on Facebook. Suddenly, there were photos, lots of photos, with her friends, her family. And she was glowing.

She had new glasses, a together outfit—an emerald green sweater and jeans that fit, but not too tightly, and her hair was beautifully done.

She told me about when she officially decided to have gastric bypass surgery. The last straw was a tuna sandwich at work.

"I couldn't stop. I knew I was full, yet I plowed through that other half. I was disgusted with myself. I decided right then and there, I needed help."

She lost 130 pounds in eighteen months. Suddenly. That seemed like a long time to me, but it included a four-month plateau owing to the cookies and holiday treats her coworkers had brought in over Christmas.

"I'd eat one cookie. But one cookie every day adds up to a lot of cookies," she said.

I thought about how many cookies I ate every week.

She admitted that sometimes she still struggled.

"Last week, I had a craving for a candy I like. I couldn't stop thinking about it. Then, the voice of my nutritionist rang in my head. I thought, Caryn, do you want the Juju Bees or the size six dress? I chose the dress," she said.

"Meat can be a problem. I have a bit of steak maybe three or four times a year. Lamb may be a problem," she said. It was just too hard to digest. It took a while for her to eat solid food again. In the beginning, she dumped, a bariatric term for vomiting.

We talked some more, me peppering her with questions, in full reporter mode. After we paid the check, she handed me a book with Al Roker on the cover. There he was: a perennial poster child for the surgery.

"I found it helpful. You might, too. If you like it, keep it. If you go another direction, just send it back," she said.

I tucked it in my bag, then picked up the car seat with Elliott, who was hungry and howling.

"Oh, one more thing. I feel incredible, and I don't fall anymore."

I don't have that problem, I thought.

Then I remembered that I had fallen in January, just a few months earlier, on a date night with Chris. We were in

New York City, and I'd been trying to keep up with him when—boom, I fell, fracturing my ankle. I wore a brace for six weeks, which wasn't easy while being a mom to two young girls and a son. It took months to recover and multiple sessions of physical therapy to regain full motion in the joint.

So I did fall. I had just been too embarrassed to remember.

◇◇◇

I learned I won a book award. So, that night, in a festive mood, we ordered dinner from the Greek Grill. My husband and I each got our usual: Greek salads to split in half, saving the other half for lunch the following day. The meat on top was lamb gyro.

"Mmm," I said. How could I live with just a piece or two of this? I popped another sliver in my mouth and took a moment to appreciate how perfectly seasoned it was. How tender it was. How the fat caressed my tongue as I rolled it in my mouth. "That is so, so good."

I hadn't told Chris about what Caryn said—how lamb might be an issue after the procedure. I wanted that to be my problem. For now, I wanted to enjoy what I was eating, in the moment, in case it was my last chance.

I had felt this way before, like something was my last chance just as I started another diet or on the Sunday night before I started a regimen of protein drinks. This feeling, this sentiment, just led to binging.

But this time, I wasn't doing it alone. I was simply eating a meal with my family. Then, we opened an artisanal-chocolate-covered Champagne bottle that I had received as a thank-you for speaking at a women's conference; it came complete with chocolate-rimmed glasses. It had been chilling in the fridge, waiting for the right moment. This seemed as good as any. Chris popped the cork off the back porch, and it landed solidly in the neighbor's yard, somewhere near their playhouse, then he poured the bubbly into the chocolate-rimmed glasses. Everything was so beautiful and decadent looking, I wanted to go through the whole bottle in a single sitting, not bit by bit, chipping away at it until it was just pieces of jagged chocolate. A whole bottle to be consumed by the two of us.

We broke up the chocolate and put it out on the table for the kids to share.

"This is good chocolate," Chris said. Chris is rarely enthusiastic about chocolate.

It far surpassed the hollow bunny I'd eaten earlier in the week. It had been a month since Easter and because it was just sitting around, I finished it off.

And then I felt hollow afterward, like the bunny. But enjoying this chocolate with my husband was true bliss. Something I didn't allow myself to feel when I binged alone in the quiet, dark moments of night to drown out the screaming anxiety in my mind.

I could taste every molecule of the milk chocolate. The white chocolate. The two melded together in my mouth in a sensual reunion. Would I be able to enjoy this kind of pleasure after the surgery? My mind swirled with what-ifs. What if I could lose the weight on my own? What if Chris was right and surgery was a bad idea?

I had already asked this question in the doctor's office and the surgeon told me that a few patients had second thoughts, canceled the surgery, then ultimately came back after putting on even more weight.

My uncertainty fed my anxiety—which fed my appetite. I was glad that by the end of the evening, we'd eaten all the chocolate and it wouldn't be hanging around the following day to soothe me. Because it couldn't.

The next day, when I woke up, I told Chris, "I dreamed I was running with you."

"You could run with me now," he said.

"In my dream, I could keep up. I was lighter, freer."

He looked down at his leftover spaghetti and meat-balls, rewarmed in the microwave.

"Have you been binging during the day?" he asked.

I knew that he knew. He'd left the empty Rice Krispies bar box on the counter instead of putting it in the recy-cling, as if for evidence.

"It has been a rough week," I said, and then I took a deep breath and added, "I've been approved for the surgery. I'm going to go for it."

He was quiet. But he nodded—it would be okay. He could see me suffering. He knew this is what would, or could, help me.

The next months before the surgery in the fall were filled with appointments. I needed to see a cardiologist, have an organ scan, see my general practitioner, and more, along with being a writer and a mom.

I spooned a mix of rice cereal and peas into Elliott's mouth. He was five months and just starting to get his first taste of solid food after a liquid diet of breastmilk and formula. I wondered how long I would have to go without solid food. I would have to relearn to eat—the same types of puréed foods Elliott was eating. Baby food. Baby steps.

My jeans, size twenty-eight, which had once been somewhat roomy on me, felt tight everywhere. I blamed the fact that they just came out of the dryer, but I didn't remember them coming out this tight before. I hadn't changed our dryer settings. What was changing was me. I was getting bigger.

Just that weekend, when I kicked off my shoe, something popped.

"Haaaaaaaah." I cringed, grasping my knee with one hand and holding on to the door jamb with the other.

"What's wrong, Mom?" Anna asked.

I tried not to let her see my eyes watering, but I wasn't sure I could walk. The last thing I needed was another trip to the hospital. I thought about my upcoming hospital stay after surgery. Two days. A two-day stay in a hospital would be a kind of break. A little vacation from life. But there could be no hospital stay for this knee injury. After I limped over to the table for lunch—a peanut butter and jelly sandwich—my knee popped back into place, leaving me sweaty and a bit out of breath.

I wondered when it would happen again.

Maybe soon. Maybe never.

◇◇◇

With three kids, Chris and I were outnumbered. We needed help.

"I sat next to the loveliest Swedish au pair," my mother-in-law told me when she brought the girls home from swimming lessons. That was it, I thought. I went online and immediately began clicking through AuPair Care profiles.

I wanted an au pair who was qualified and who didn't

look like a *Sports Illustrated* model. I trusted my husband, but at three hundred pounds, I didn't feel like tempting fate. I decided on Pauline, a young woman from France, who, when I interviewed her over Skype, seemed competent, kind, motivated, and really a hard worker. She was pretty, with dark brown hair that framed her face, and was sturdy, too: not too heavy and not too thin. She had strong, healthy arms and legs, and she exuded a body confidence and style that I wanted to impart to my daughters. In one of her videos, she slid down a slide with one of her young charges. I couldn't fit on a slide. She'd be able to keep up with our kids in ways that I couldn't.

When she arrived in our home, not the condo but a fixer-upper we'd purchased a year ago, she burst into tears. Maybe it was our creaky floors? Maybe our place was not exactly the vision of American opulence she had imagined. I had worked for weeks to get her room ready, and my mother had even come down from Vermont to help me organize. I was so proud of converting her bathroom from Spartan man-john to a clean, white commode, complete with subway tile, just like on HGTV. But I had to admit: many things in our home were a little bit broken. The paint was peeling from the attic ceiling. The kitchen faucet leaked. The toilet downstairs tended to clog for no apparent reason.

Or maybe it was me.

I wondered if my weight contributed to her initial re-action. After all, I was part of the reason the floors creaked; they practically buckled under my weight.

Pauline's unhappiness wasn't the only problem. Having an extra person in our house made me even more self-conscious about myself as a person and as a parent. I imagined she thought I was a terrible mother. Or perhaps she'd announce she wanted to leave.

I hired someone from France because Anna had been enamored with the country since a family trip there, and, on video at least, Pauline seemed perfect. Secretly, I hoped that her French eating style would rub off on me. I had read *French Women Don't Get Fat,* and I thought she could be a good influence.

As it turned out, she ate Nutella sandwiches for break-fast and had an affinity for 5 Guys Burgers. I had to de-cide whether it was okay to have Nutella in the house; a relationship with chocolate hazelnut spread should not be complicated, but for me it was.

You see, first, I started buying it by the cute little jelly-jar size. Then, as the kids asked for it every day on their toast (when in Rome, right?), I moved up to the commercial, crepe-making size. Then, I started putting a lump in my cof-fee each day. That's when we got a Costco membership and I bought it in bulk. And I was totally okay with that.

Until I wasn't.

◇◇◇

Later, Pauline told me, not in an insulting way, that she hadn't believed how fat I was, that she didn't realize it when we Skyped or when she saw images of me. Photos of me, which are mostly from the waist up, make me look somewhat normal sized. On the date of her arrival, it was mostly homesickness that overtook her, she admitted. She was close to her family, had a beautiful relationship, and would miss them.

I wanted to get to know her better. On one of the first days she was there, I asked her what she liked to do.

"I like to do tree climbing," she said.

Could that really be a thing? "Do you mean ropes courses?"

"Yes, yes. Ropes," she said. "And roller . . ."

"Roller skating," I said. "Actually, that's the roller-skating rink right there." I pointed across the intersection at the eighties-style fortress called Florham Park Roller Rink. "We've never actually been there."

I thought about the times Chris had suggested it and I'd changed the subject or begged for another activity. I worried I would fall and, with wheels on my feet, be unable to raise my rump from the shellacked floor. It struck me that our new au pair had just named two activities I didn't feel comfortable doing anymore. That I couldn't do any more. I mean, sure, I *could,* but the results might be disastrous. What would Anna think of her mother, all tangled up in her own skates, trying to hoist herself up? Would she pretend not to know me or would she come and help? I wasn't sure I wanted to know the answer.

I thought about Pauline doing all those things—a ropes course, skating, and skiing with my kids, maybe Chris, too—and my heart sank straight into my stomach. *Kaplunk.* I had to admit that I'd hired an au pair to do all the active-mom things I couldn't. Because I had rendered myself unable. Too heavy for any of it.

Was I about to replace myself? Was I making it obvious to my husband that he could have someone more active? (As if he didn't know that already.) That my girls could have a mother who could do active things, who could hold their hands at the skating rink? Even if I wanted to do a ropes course, I exceeded the weight limit.

So much for our getting-to-know-you conversation. I could already tell that my new au pair was perplexed by my weight. Already I had munched through some of the candy Pauline had bought for Emily and Anna. Every time I went by the cabinet, I thought about it sitting there. It was blatantly obvious from the moment she arrived that my new au pair was way better at taking care of herself than I was.

"Where is the iron?" she asked one day.

"Up here," I said, pulling it out of the closet. "I never use it."

"You never use?"

"I should, but I don't," I said. I felt momentarily embarrassed that I sent my kids out in public in wrinkled clothes. But that was why she was there. I needed help. Now I was getting it, but I had never felt so self-conscious about my weight and our lifestyle habits.

One day, driving home with Pauline, I spotted a Boston Market and decided to get us both a chicken sandwich for lunch.

"What is mac and cheese?" she asked.

"Pasta with cheese," I said. I was trying to be good, so I ordered sweet potatoes as a side, then waited as the drive-through person handed over our sodas.

"Wow, they're big," Pauline said.

"Yes, American sizes." I shrugged.

She got a Coke, and I was compelled to say, "I don't really drink soda anymore. I used to drink diet soda, but I stopped when I was pregnant. I didn't really want it any more. It didn't taste the same." Experts often pointed at soda for our nation's epidemic of obesity. I felt like I needed to tell the world that I didn't drink soda. It was one of the only things I denied myself.

"But sometimes, I have lemonade," I said, tearing off the end of the wrapper and plunging my straw in, making the liquid spill out. "Oops." I blushed, trying to mop it up before it landed on my seatbelt extender or Pauline's pants.

When we returned home, Elliott was still asleep, re-covering from his recent immunizations. I lifted his car seat into the living room and got some plates for our lunch, hoping that would make it fancier, even with our large soft drinks on the side.

"Good meal," she said.

"Yes, *bon appétit.*"

I felt silly saying that over takeout. There was no ju-lienne, no fresh-baked anything. Just a fast-food chicken sandwich because I didn't want to bother spending the time to make something for lunch.

But maybe Pauline's presence was just what I needed, because I found myself eating only three-quarters of my sandwich and wrapping the rest in paper for later. I kind of loved having Pauline supervise me. I never trusted myself with food.

I hated it, too. Every time I was in the kitchen, she knew. She was the one who did the dishes. She knew if there was an extra spoon. If I snuck in there at night, she surely heard my footsteps in her bedroom below.

I wanted to tell her about my surgery, but I worried what she would think. I wasn't ready to tell her, or most people. Not yet.

The presurgery psychiatrist shared a building with a Rita's Italian Ice shop.

Was this part of the test?

I had fifteen minutes to spare before my appointment, which meant I had time for a snack. Then I decided that the best test for me would be to wait it out. To try to resist until the end of my appointment. In the waiting room, headline news blared. Then-presidential candidate *Donald Trump isn't a racist,* New Jersey governor Chris Christie declared. I looked at his girth and snarkily wondered how his lap band was working, then chided myself for being so judgy. I wondered if I could explore this with the psychiatrist.

The chairs in the waiting room were narrow, and I wondered how some of the heaviest of patients could sit there, especially because this office had been recommended for my pre-bariatric-surgery psych evaluation. My hips were poking through the wooden slots, and the arm rests sealed my thighs together. All this clenching and squeezing put pressure on my bladder. I had to pee even though I had gone right before I entered the office.

Forty-five minutes passed.

"Is it usually this long of a wait?" I asked the woman next to me.

"Not usually. She's a very good doctor," she said. "Very good."

When I arrived, there were four people ahead of me. Each session lasted about fifteen minutes. I wondered how people could talk about their feelings in just fifteen minutes. When it was my turn, she asked me some basics about my job, my age, my children. How long I had tried to drop pounds. What I'd tried.

As she questioned, my eyes zeroed in on the jar of candy on her desk, full of Jolly Ranchers, which I didn't even like. But there were mini Milky Way and Snickers bars mixed in there, too.

Was this part of the test? I wondered. What would she think if I helped myself to the candy? Should I just do it, or should I ask first? As she talked, my eyes darted back and forth between her lips and the candy jar, and I only looked away when she handed me a list of questions meant to gauge whether I was depressed. *Do you ever feel guilty about overeating? Do you ever feel like hurting yourself?*

At the moment, I didn't feel depressed. I was feeling excited about the possibilities, about a new life. I wanted to tell her what she wanted to hear so she would recommend the surgery. So I lied. When she asked if I binged, I said only sometimes, trying to not let on that I did it every day. I wanted this surgery.

I *was* prepared to talk about my past, the reasons I started using food to soothe myself in the first place—from my parents' divorce to being molested on my twelfth birthday, but she didn't ask much.

"You should get the surgery," she concluded. "Your doctor is a good surgeon. One of the best," she said. "But if you start to think about binging or actually do it, you need to talk to someone right away before it becomes a problem. And there's this. . . ." She handed me a brochure for a medication aimed at helping people who struggle with Binge Eating Disorder. "It isn't approved yet, but it will be available soon."

"Thank you," I said. I thought I was getting this procedure so I wouldn't need diet pills. I was a little confused.

She didn't ask me if I had any fears about the procedure—about dying and leaving my life, friends, and family behind. Or my fear that, at my core, I would always be the same person. That no surgery could change that.

That I would still be a less-than-perfect parent.

That I would still be afraid of my body. My appetite.

That I would always have an emotional hole in my heart but that after surgery I wouldn't be able to use food to patch it.

She didn't ask if I worried that, unable to eat like I had before, I might become an outcast at my own dining table, drinking shakes while everyone else scarfed down steaks and bread. She didn't ask about the anxiety I felt, always, about eating the wrong things. She didn't ask if I worried that my skin would look like a saggy elephant's after dropping a hundred pounds.

That people may not recognize me.

That, after all this, I may be empty. Completely empty. The person who can't think of anything to say at a dinner party.

That, other than my husband, no one has said, not one time, "No, you don't need to get the surgery." No one has tried to talk me out of it. Not even her.

After the appointment, I rewarded myself by walking around the building to the Italian ice shop, as I knew I would. I wondered if the office staff could see me from their windows. I wondered if they wagered on which patients would end up there.

"Hey there, what can I get you today?"

I scanned the menu. I wasn't looking for a healthy treat.

"A Heath Bar milkshake," I said.

"Excellent choice," she said.

Really, I thought. Nice of her to say, but probably not the best for me. Still, I wanted it.

As she blended it all together, I scanned the board for something I might be able to have after the procedure. I saw a single sugar-free option. Peach-strawberry something. It didn't tempt me now. Would I want it after?

"Would you like whipped cream and a cherry?"

"Yes," I said. "Yes, I would."

*I*t was time for my appointment with the nutritionist—or, as people on bariatric surgery chat boards call them, my "Nut."

Her assistant was heavy. She wore a pretty royal blue top. As I filled out the paperwork, I wondered where she shopped. I also wondered whether it bothered the nutritionist that her assistant was heavy. Or did it bother the assistant that her boss was a nutritionist? I can't listen to too-skinny nutritionists without thinking they must be suffering from some kind of eating disorder; I wondered if the assistant had similar thoughts.

But this Nut was nice. Her name was Sara, and she seemed smart and approachable. She asked me to sit down in her white, windowless office. She sat in front of a small Apple computer and ran through a few questions and my medical history, and then started to dig in about food.

"So, what time do you have breakfast?"

I detailed my usual routine, starting with toast "and sometimes Nutella." I said *sometimes,* though I had it multiple times a day, every day.

"You do know that Nutella isn't the same thing as peanut butter?"

"Unfortunately, I do," I said.

"Just making sure because some people think the hazelnuts in there make it a protein source."

"No, I'm clear that it's just for recreational use," I said. "I do like Triple X yogurt."

"You mean Triple Zero," she said, with a little smirk. She knew it well because it had zero fat, zero added sugars, a hit with her bariatric clientele.

"Oh, right. I guess Triple X would be a whole different kind of yogurt," I said.

We laughed. She seemed human. Not just some robot doling out healthy living advice, treating me like a body size that wasn't right. In other words, I liked her.

Still, I couldn't tell her the truth about Nutella. We were going through a tub of Nutella once a week, and I happily allowed it, with the excuse that it kept my au pair happy. But it kept me happy as well.

Then she mentioned quitting carbs in the evening even before the surgery.

"I don't know if my husband or kids will go for that," I said.

"You have a heavy influence on how your family eats," she said. "Eating is a learned behavior. And you teach your children how to do it." She must have seen my face—guilty as charged—because she continued, detailing a faux pas of her own. "One day my little guy got hurt and I found myself saying, 'Oh, sweetie, do you want a cookie?' And I'm a nutritionist! If our kids have a bad day, we take them for ice cream. We're the ones who teach them that."

I had done that as well. I liked that she told me her story. It can be instinctual to offer food when someone is in pain. But it's an instinct we have to fight.

"I eat mostly healthy foods, I guess. I just don't have an off switch," I said.

"Some people still struggle with that after the procedure," she said. "Most of your work will be in your mind. It sounds kind of crazy, but you'll have to talk to yourself a lot, like if you find yourself in front of the refrigerator and you open it looking for something to eat. You'll have to ask yourself, *What am I doing here? How is this food going to make me feel?* Chances are, whatever it is you want to eat in the moment will make you feel crummy afterward, and whatever was bothering you will still be there. The trick is to find out what you can do to make whatever is bothering you better—without food."

She explained that I'd have to be on a liquid diet for a week or two before the surgery, to shrink my liver, which can get in the way of the stomach. I wasn't sure I could stick to a liquid diet for a week, much less two. I wondered if my surgeon would know if I cheated.

She went on to describe the clear liquid diet I'd be on for the first few days after surgery, followed by ordinary liquids for a week and then puréed foods. Ricotta cheese, yogurt, tuna, and white fish would be good during this time. After accidentally putting a spoonful of chicken and brown rice purée to my mouth instead of my son's, I was grateful to hear that.

"You'll probably want to wait six to eight weeks for fresh vegetables—though some people try at four weeks," she said.

I thought about my garden, which I had groomed and tended. By that point, two months after surgery, it would be closed for the season.

"And then from then on," she continued, "it's lean proteins first and low carbs, from then on. You want to follow these rules to avoid vomiting as much as possible. Otherwise, the stomach could split open."

I imagined my stomach bursting and all my food spilling inside because I ate the wrong things, such as toast. I loved the smell of toast. How could I live without it?

"Once you're a bariatric patient. You're always a bariatric patient," she said.

I know. I know, I thought. But did I really?

"I don't think anyone likes me," Anna said. Then she turned back to her Harry Potter book, her fourth in the series since she started reading them two weeks prior.

"Of course they do," I told her. Earlier that day, she had a play date with a friend. I reminded her of that.

"But in school," she said. "No one likes to talk with me."

I knew how she felt. The emptiness of being the person no one wanted to know or touch. The one too big to hug. Sometimes, I wondered whether other mothers weren't allowing their kids to come play with Anna because of me. Were they worried that I'd feed their kids a buffet of sweets? Did they think I was a bad influence?

Recently, the mother of one of Anna's friends pumped me full of questions—about who was bothering Anna at school and about my weight. After, it seemed she didn't want to send her daughter over to our house anymore. The friend's birthday came and went without an invitation for Anna, though we had invited her to Anna's party. Was my daughter being blacklisted? Was I?

After all, I was a mess, shaky from my coffee in the morning after nights of being constantly awakened by my kids. The morning of one of the first days of a new school year, I lost my mind after having to chase down the toddler to put her hair tie in. I soothed myself with Nutella, stirring it into my coffee, then plopped the spoon with the unmelted remainder in my mouth. My moment of calm before the crush of trying to get the girls to school on time. But the habit only made me more agitated with myself in the long run.

I had all the green lights for surgery, but I was still a wreck when it came to food—and I knew the surgery wasn't going to solve it. I was still in the perpetual cycle of starting the day on a diet and ending it in failure, even with the surgery date looming. At each checkup, the doctors suggested I start dropping pounds, but I didn't, even though I ordered four different kinds of protein powders to try. I had them with everything else, even Nutella. I had to heal my mind somehow.

My friend Jennifer, who'd also done the surgery, had advice for me. "You will be the same after surgery. The only thing different will be the size of your stomach. Make sure you keep going to a therapist."

I needed to find someone who knew a thing or two about binge eating.

I called my husband's mental health benefits line again. I was looking for someone who specialized in binge eating, even if I didn't want to call what I did an eating disorder. In my mind, people with eating disorders were anorexics and bulimics.

I'd heard a few different terms floating around for what I struggled with: compulsive overeating, food addiction. But there was a new-ish diagnosis that seemed to fit the bill, one that fifteen-minute psychiatrist had mentioned: Binge Eating Disorder. I fit all the symptoms: frequent overeating that felt compulsive and out of control, followed by overwhelming shame, guilt, and embarrassment.

Having a name for what I was going through was a huge relief. Food wasn't just food to me. I binged to push away anything bad—or good. I ate to forget. I ate to remember. I forgot when I ate. I remembered that I was a failure at something as simple as eating.

I had been in therapy before. After I was molested, I worked with someone who let me tell my story through Tarot cards (even though I was hoping for a better outcome for my future. A boyfriend. Fortune. Fame like Tiffany or Debbi Gibson). After Anna was born, I saw a therapist who specialized in eating disorders but who was more geared toward anorexia and bulimia. The chairs in her waiting room were certainly designed for that population. The love seat, which would have fit only my rear, was often shared by an anorexic and her mother. I stood, feeling uncomfortable, while waiting for my session.

So I was skeptical when the health insurance folks pointed me to Marnie Grossman, a psychotherapist based in Millburn, just one town away. Her office turned out to be an oasis. My travel bug heart gleamed when I saw the *National Geographic* covers framed along the back wall. The Pier 1 cabinet with the Buddha's head on top.

Marnie's hair was beautiful, curling past her shoulders in a natural, effortless-looking wave. I couldn't remember whether I had brushed my hair that day. Still, she was easy to talk to. "Why are you here today?" she asked, with a kind smile.

I grabbed the fat on one of my thighs, which hung over the seat. The wide armchair barely fit me, but I needed the arms and table in front of it to get up again. I worried I would have sunk too deeply into the couch.

"I know this is the past," I said. "And this is too," grabbing the fat on my belly. I rarely touched my own belly in front of anyone. But there I was, yanking at my flab as if I was offering it to her.

She scribbled some notes, trying to get some of my history down on paper.

"Siblings?"

I told her about my brothers, my close relationship with my brother Derek and my more complicated one with Bryan. I told her that it was his friend who sexually assaulted me and that, afterward, he still hung out with the guy, even though the guy wasn't allowed in our house. Even now, Bryan was Facebook friends with him.

We talked about the recent binging I'd been doing as I supposedly prepared for surgery. "I'm just worried I won't be able to eat these things after September."

"So, this is a farewell," she said.

"Yes, a culinary farewell tour, I guess. But like the Eagles, I'll be back, just older, wiser, and at a higher cost."

We laughed.

"Listen, we can talk about some heavy stuff in here. You have to have humor to balance it out," she said.

I liked her.

"What's different is how you deal with things. Without food, you'll have to deal with things. I'd like to talk about your brother, your father, maybe a little bit about your mother."

"Okay," I said.

"Okay."

Deal with things.

That afternoon, I put things into place before starting my chili. I lined up the spices on the counter—chili, cumin, and paprika. I stacked the cans of beans and crushed tomatoes so they looked like a wall along the windowsill, where a tomato from my garden was ripening. I stretched the plastic webbed bag of the onions so it snapped open and three onions tumbled out onto the electric blue cutting board, which was scored with knife marks from many meals made before this one.

I cut the onions, first lopping off the ends, then peeling off the outer layer of skin, and dicing them until I had a mound ready for the pot. My eyes welled up and spilled over.

I was making an extra batch in case I didn't feel like making chili after the surgery. I thought that if I didn't survive, at least there would be something for my family to eat.

I wanted to throw the perfect party to say goodbye to food as I knew it. And to be with friends. The thought did cross my mind that I might not ever see them again. Immediately, I started Googling bouncy houses. I wanted to turn the backyard into a carnival. In Summit, parties are an opportunity to impress, to make the kids call out their parents for their inadequacies.

The previous year, when I was super-pregnant with Elliot and aiming to please my girls, I said yes when Anna asked for a Halloween party. I made pumpkin chili and "rigaboni" and decked out the dining room in orange and black. I carved a frickin' cauliflower into a skull for the vegetable platter and a watermelon into a monster face for the fruit plate. I was feeling pretty Pinterest proud until the kids discovered the Goldfish in our pantry and started going to town on all our snacks for the week.

The next day, our neighbors, who couldn't be nicer, threw a Halloween party at their house. They had a face painter and a balloon artist, and the food was catered. They also had a playhouse. (I couldn't compete, so after that I decided to hold off on future Halloween parties.)

I had pestered Chris about getting a grill, since most of our neighbors had one, usually a Weber. Although that was outside of our budget, I got Chris a Home Depot card for Father's Day so he could ultimately decide on the best deal. We used it on Labor Day for what I thought of as my last barbecue with an intact stomach. I dreamed of going to the Meat House, a local butcher, and getting the finest cuts of meat to share with friends.

"Why don't we just get some nice burgers?" Chris asked. "I mean, it's a barbeque. That's all people will expect."

But this was part of my farewell tour to food as I knew it. I envisioned an evening with friends, partly mourning my relationship with food or pre-mourning if I didn't make it through the surgery. There would be five guests, my inner circle, the only people I told about the procedure.

It was nice to be around such supportive friends. What I thought would be a solemn occasion turned out to be one of love and support. With good meat.

As I held my hamburger—sirloin, grilled medium-rare—I wondered if this would be the last time I'd be able to deliver a hamburger to my mouth this way, in a fluffy bun. At future barbecues, would I ask for one without a bun? What if there were no forks and knives out? Should I keep them in my purse just in case?

"Are you nervous? Excited?" My friends asked me about the surgery, sweetly, in many ways. I told them I just wanted to enjoy the food I had. To make good choices. To be glad to be around the people who loved me as I was. Who loved me enough not to discourage me from having surgery. To know that was the best I could do for myself.

Chris offered me a cookie, from a tray he balanced on the palm of his hand, like a waiter. "Your last one for a while," he said with a coy smile. I chose a white chocolate and macadamia nut, better than chocolate chip to me.

As the sun dipped below the trees and friends started to gather their little ones home for bedtime, I cleaned up the yard. I was one day closer to surgery and grateful for the friends and family supporting me. There were no "you're fine the way you are" or other comments. They knew I needed help. They could see that I'd become a shell of the active person I once was. How hard it was for me to get up out of a chair. How stressed and bewildered I looked at a restaurant. And perhaps, until now, they didn't quite know how to tell me their concerns.

◇◇◇

I'd been counting on my mother, who had promised to come for my surgery. Except my stepfather was scheduled

for surgery to deal with an aneurism in his abdomen a full
month after mine.

"I can't make it," she told me. "I feel like these are Lee's
last days. I can feel him pulling away from me. And I know
you're going to make it through this. I know you will."

"I know, Mom. I understand."

But I didn't. I knew she was hurting, but I wanted to
tell her that I was hurting, too. "I'm sending you two meditation CDs to prep for surgery. I can be there for you over
the phone. I know I miss a lot of things," she said.

She really did. She'd promised to come down so many
times, then hadn't, that I could only conclude I wasn't
worth the trip.

But I was taking a drastic step, after three decades of
abusing my body.

I couldn't keep quiet. "I'm scared and I'm really disappointed," I burst out. "I know that probably doesn't change
the situation, but I need to tell you that because it's the
truth." I started to sob. Mom just listened to me weep.

"I know I'll be okay, I'll be better than I've ever been,
but I'm scared and I really wanted you to be there . . . and
here we are again, with you telling me that you won't be
able to make it," I said. Suddenly, I couldn't talk anymore,
I couldn't cry anymore. "I have to go, Mom. I have some
work to do."

Saying what I needed to say felt as if something exited
my body, fell off my shoulders.

The next morning, my mother called.

"Lee is insisting that I come. I will be there," she said.

My instinct was to say, "Oh, Mom, you don't have to."

But I wanted her to come more than anything.

This is when I felt my head nuzzle into her shoulder even though she wasn't there. Suddenly, I felt completely and utterly loved. As if I was glowing with it. And I knew that I would be okay.

That night, I dreamed that I was sweaty, horsing around on the basketball court with Chris. I woke up refreshed, feeling wonderful. I hadn't played basketball with him in years. Perhaps a decade. But it was how we used to hang out.

We'd play HORSE, though we nicknamed it WHORES because we could be naughty like that. And he'd always win, though I always wagered. The loser—me—had to pick up the dinner tab, but I loved to play with him.

We laughed about whiffing our shots, when the ball didn't even go up to the rim and went straight past. Later, though we spent eight years living next to basketball courts, we didn't play again. Our basketball just sat, deflated, in the closet for nearly a decade.

Now, I couldn't wait to lose to him again in real life. To be a player again.

Anxiety practically vibrated out of my body. I had to calm down.

I had ordered a maple bourbon pecan pie and steak tips for my last meal before surgery.

I messaged Julia. "I'm so anxious I can't even stand it."

"Embrace it," she replied. "From here on out you'll lose two pounds a day. Be excited."

I tried to be excited, but my body wasn't.

I went out to the bakery to pick up the pie and there was Carolyn, another person who had weight loss surgery four years ago. I confessed about the pecan pie because she would understand more than anyone.

"I totally get it. Last supper syndrome. I did it too," she said. "It's going to be okay. This kind of surgery is so routine now. You're going to be just fine.

"I just workout all the time now. I'm crazy cranky if I don't get a workout in. You'll see. Your whole world will change and it's going to be awesome," she said. "I'll check in with you next week, but you're going to be fine."

She was right. I was going to be fine. I was going to be *great*.

But I still felt guilty about the pie.

When I got home, I rifled through everything in my kitchen. Surely, there was something I wanted to eat. A handful of Lucky Charms. A spoonful of Nutella. Each one of these grabs of food only disgusted me more.

I saw the three dark green zucchinis on my counter. I thought about how much my little ones love my fritters.

I thought about the stockpile of chili I had in the freezer. It was already made.

I cut a piece of pie and ate it immediately. It was runnier than I remembered. Then again, maybe there was no such thing as a perfect last meal. Maybe I didn't need a last meal. I would still be able to have pecans, though perhaps not in this form.

And in two months, I'd be able to have steak, the more tender, the better. What was I worried about? I hadn't had a good steak in two months, maybe six. So why all the hurry to have one last binge for the ages?

What I really needed was a plan for success after surgery. A job outside the house so that I didn't spend half the day circling the kitchen. A therapist. I liked Marnie and had already arranged another appointment. But I was still anxious. I texted Chris my usual: *ETA?* I hoped he'd be home earlier than usual so we could enjoy my last meal. I unloaded the haul from Meat House and spread everything out on the counter. Forty-one dollars' worth of steak, two loaves of bread, and sweet potatoes. In the fridge, there was a maple bourbon pecan pie. Tonight's meal would be special.

◇◇◇

"Don't worry about me, I'll have the chicken and pasta," Pauline said.

"But it's steak," I said, pointing to the tender slabs.

Emily stuck her tongue out.

Anna belted out Pink songs so she could curse.

Emily screamed and ran from the table. "I hate this!"

"Please. Please. I'm trying to have a special meal. Tonight is the last night Mommy can have real food for a while." I tried to look at my meat, which by now was cold.

"Blah," Emily said, before emitting a wail. She stuck her tongue out again, only to lick the meat.

Then Elliott cried and my attention was diverted from my own meal to spooning food into his mouth.

"Oh, come on people," I muttered.

"Can I have a bite of your bread?" Anna said, reaching for the slice and spreading it with a liberal swath of butter. "Is it time for pie yet?" she asked.

"Sure, you can grab it," I said to Anna, trying to shovel in a few more bites of steak. Emily grabbed a Klondike bar instead. I had wanted this to be a long, lingering, candlelit meal. Now I was just trying to get through it without another outburst.

Suddenly, I felt full, too full, like the food was going to come back up my throat.

I spent the day before surgery relaxing, making sure my hospital bag was packed with cozy clothes to wear home—essentially, yoga pants—and lip balm. I had to wash before bed, go to sleep on clean sheets, wear clean pajamas, and wash once more with special surgery soap in the morning.

My surgery wasn't until the afternoon, so I could sleep in and relax in the morning . . . without a single thing in my stomach.

It was empty and ready to be severed.

I insisted on driving so I wouldn't get carsick and felt in control. I was already nervous as it was. Chris sat in the front passenger seat, and my mom sat in the back. My in-laws had the kids, and I cranked up Nina Simone's "Feeling Good" as I started the engine. "It's a new day, it's a new dawn. It's a new life for me," I sang, with hope.

Chris quickly realized what I was listening to and popped the CD out.

"We don't want to be listening to the *Six Feet Under* album," he said. I guess he was nervous, too. But I liked it because of the Nina Simone song. I'd played it a lot when I lost 120 pounds.

While I was being prepped for surgery, Mom and Chris went out for lunch. Chris came back with a Jimmy John's sub drink cup. I wasn't jealous at all.

The nurse gave me something to drink in a little cup. She said it was so my stomach muscles would relax. I think it was for me to relax, too. There, waiting for surgery, I was calm, peaceful, and ready. Given my normal anxiety level, I deduced that I was somewhat sedated. That was a good thing.

I had red hospital socks, the kind with treads on both sides so I wouldn't slip.

"You have Christmas socks," Chris said, flipping up my sheet and tickling my right foot.

I gave him a half smile and didn't yank my foot back.

Dr. Danny, the anesthesiologist, entered the cubicle.

"I like to use my patients' first names when they wake up," he said. "Is that okay with you, Care-ah?"

"Yes, but it's Kahr-ah."

"Kara like Super Girl. You are Super Girl. Any questions?"

"What if I have to go to the bathroom?"

"You won't," he said.

I felt like it was too late to ask anything. Everyone was there to support me, my mother, and Chris, and it felt right. I wasn't afraid.

"Okay, it's time to go," he said. He wheeled me through the hospital.

"We're now on the other side of Middlesex County," he said. It was all jovial until we entered the operating room.

My eyes darted from table to table. I saw sharp instruments. They wheeled my gurney right next to the operating table and asked me to scooch on. I panicked.

"We're going to take good care of you," a person in scrubs and a blue hat said. "This will be super-fast," he added.

Under the lights, I could hear my heart racing. No matter what sedative they'd given me, I wanted to go, to get off the table.

"Are we ready for a time-out?" Danny asked.

The surgical coordinator from Dr. Sadek's office started to read out my particulars.

"Here we have Kara Richardson Whitely, age forty-two, for a gastric sleeve, possible open. We have blood available if needed," she said.

When she finished, I could hear Dr. Danny adjusting one of his machines.

"Okay, Kara, my medicine burns a little on its way in. But in a moment, you won't feel a thing," he said.

"*OW,*" I said and then I was out.

Chris left to get my clear protein drinks, figuring I'd be a while. Mom hung tight. Within thirty minutes—possibly even twenty—Dr. Sadek was out to tell her everything was fine.

"*Kara.*

"*Kara,* you're all finished. You did a great job," Dr. Danny told me, as he wheeled me to recovery.

My mouth was so cottony. All I wanted was ice chips. I opened my eyes to see Chris.

Damn, he's handsome, I thought. Then I saw my mother moving her hands above me in Healing Touch, a holistic practice to draw away any pain and encourage the body to heal.

"The doctor said you did great, sweetie," Chris said. He stood up to hold my hand. "Just rest now."

I dozed in and out. Until it was time to get up and walk. Walking would help release the gas the surgeons used to blow up the belly and make room for their instruments.

"Up, down, the only way you'll feel better is if you walk it out," my nurse said. She seemed very young and eager to help me. I stood up, with Chris on one side and my mom on the other, and felt so dizzy I needed a moment. I got about ten feet down the hallway and felt like I was going to collapse.

I put my hand on my back, making sure my gown was closed. My IV with a slow drip of morphine trailed behind. "I'm not quite sure I'm awake yet." I imagined falling, my stomach bursting open, and the IV yanking out of my arm. We turned back, but as we rounded the corner and approached my room, I woke up.

"Let's do this," I said to Chris. He held one arm, and I held on to the IV, the same way we did when I was in labor and we tried to get our babies to make their way down. This time, it was about getting the gas out. We took our time, but we made it around once and decided to give it a go for a second time.

By the time I arrived at my room, I was feeling much better.

Chris fed me ice chips, just as he had each time I was in labor, even though I was perfectly capable of doing it myself. I felt so taken care of, so loved in that vulnerable moment.

By morning, I was doing six laps at a time, and looking forward to Robin and my mom's arrival. Meanwhile, I was cleared to try my first liquid food—sugar-free Italian ice.

"Little by little," the nurse said. She put a tiny medicine cup in front of me . . . no bigger than an ounce. "Start slow."

The first sip made my stomach twinge. I worked on that little cup for an hour.

Mom and Robin arrived and took me home. I held the girls close to me in a gentle hug before they went off to stay at Robin's so I could recover.

My stomach was a little cranky, and it took hours to finish a twenty-ounce clear protein drink, but I wasn't in pain, and because my kids were at Robin's house, my mother and I headed for the local nursery. She bought me fall plants, perennial herbs—chives, sage, and thyme. She made it a point to get them in the ground before she left, teaching me how to press firmly around each plant to settle it into the soil. Then she yanked out the kale bushes, which were laden with whiteflies, and got rid of them. My garden looked neat and tidy for the first time all season.

*C*hris's birthday came one week after my surgery, when I was still consuming only clear liquids. He suggested the all-you-can-eat sushi restaurant that had just opened in town. "We should have done this before my surgery," I joked, but wasn't really joking.

I looked over the menu, which seemed to go on like a magazine. *What if you just try a dumpling?* I thought. *What's the worst that could happen?* Then I talked myself out of anything that wasn't prescribed and landed on a place I'd rarely settled before—broth.

It felt so sad. Everyone else was rattling off their dumpling orders and the kind of chicken and beef they wanted drizzled in sweet sauces and coupled with rice galore. My stomach was still tender and healing. I could only take clear liquids.

Suddenly, it felt okay that I wasn't so focused on eating that I could pay attention to my kids and to Chris. I wasn't

allowed to lift Elliott yet, but I could entertain him with
peekaboo. I could be at the restaurant and celebrate Chris.
This is what I told myself, again and again.

I asked the server to bring my soup when everyone
else was eating, but it came out first, maybe because he assumed that the large woman, her fat folding over the sides
of her chair, would order something else. I waited to eat until everyone else got their food, then silently sulked about
my cold soup while the rest of my family gorged. But not
eating as much allowed me to stop worrying about when
my meal was coming out. I had time to feed my little guy
purées and tiny little bites of food. He was learning to eat,
just as I was.

I made progress. When the time came for me to in-
gest regular liquids, not just clear, I ordered a four-ounce
sugar-free Italian Ice from a menu. Before surgery, it
would have taken me less than a minute to consume. After, it took me an hour. My stomach fluttered if I took
too many scoops too fast; two spoonfuls was too much.
I learned to take one bite at a time, to not swallow things
whole.

Chris stocked the fridge with clear protein drinks that
were god-awful but necessary to keep my energy up, and I
started to feel better, with more than twenty pounds gone
since I started the presurgery routine. But I was also grieving. I yearned to eat with wild abandon. It was going to

take some time to feel whole again without filling myself with food. Without making it the focus.

First clear liquids, then liquids, then purées, soft foods such as refried beans and yogurts, and, finally, a few bites of real food. We're talking less than an appetizer. I was convinced this would never be enough for me.

But unexpectedly it was. I had the sensation of being full.

How strange this was, to have an actual physical cue that I'd had enough. For years, I told myself that I needed more, more, and more. Now I had an internal gatekeeper. It was a beautiful feeling. For the first time in my life, I had had enough.

But this feeling of being fine didn't come with ease.

There was still an awful little voice in my mind telling me that I couldn't do this. When I stood in front of the fridge, it would whisper to me that I didn't have it in me to change.

My therapist, Marnie, emailed me. "Just checking in on you!" she wrote.

I told her I felt lighter, and I was. Suddenly, my knee didn't hurt. My back and body didn't feel so overwhelmed by food—surging with calories and sugar. I suddenly had enough.

But I knew my recovery from a life of disordered eating wouldn't be solved on the operating table. I needed someone to talk with, to sort out the ins and outs of the day instead of internally obsessing and ultimately binging my way to an oblivion. I could easily graze myself out of this surgery. It was my job to make sure I didn't—and it was Marnie's job to help me.

Twenty-eight days. That's how long I went after the surgery before I could eat solid food. It didn't feel like an accident that that's the average length of stay in rehab for many addictions.

It was enough of a break that I could notice the perfect structure of a cherry tree, dropping leaves in a soft fall breeze. I could feel the wind on my skin, how my cheeks pinched a bit when I smiled. I felt aware of a new, more vivid life.

Instead of wandering around the kitchen, I logged on to the Facebook bariatric surgery site to see what was normal, what I could eat when. I stayed hopeful as I checked out after photos. I was soon going to be one of them. Someone proudly displaying my after.

This was the first time I just had no interest in eating. I had to remember to drink my protein drinks. I never had to remind myself to eat before. Not ever.

And, of course, the pounds started to come off. I was down twenty pounds by the end of the first week; forty by the end of the first month. Chris hugged me tightly, something he had been afraid to do after the surgery, and his arms wrapped all the way around me. I could put a bath towel around me. There was a spring in my step, especially when people stopped me to say, "Kara, you look amazing."

With my phone and keys in my pocket, my pants started to sag downward—in a good way.

"Oh dear, my pants are falling down," I said to Anna.

I yanked them up, and Anna looked me up and down.

"You're going to need some new pants," she said with a little smirk.

I put my hands on my back to feel how the fat had loosened up. It was now jiggly, like it was getting ready to disembark from my body.

"Don't do that," she said. "There are people behind us."

But she was still smiling. She knew I was on a good path.

I started walking Anna to school, something I had avoided at my heaviest, mostly so other kids wouldn't point me out as they passed snickering in their cars. It counted as thirty minutes of exercise to jumpstart my morning. It was enough to get me motivated and to feel like I could check it off my list in case I didn't get to any other physical activity that day.

But I found myself wanting to do more. I felt AMAZ-ING. I organized my closet and realized that I had a set of clothes that I hadn't worn in years, almost a new wardrobe from the days when I had lost weight in the past. Wearing these clothes—fancy hiking duds, like a fitted eggplant purple pullover—made me look like a mountain girl again.

I continued walking—fast—up and around the hill, then would turn around and stride home. One day I ran into a neighbor.

"You look amazing," she said, as we fell into step together. "What are you doing?"

"Just eating less and moving more. I'm trying everything," I said, remembering Brigid said to have a canned response for this because the question would come up again and again. I tried not to let it make me feel uncomfortable because most people knew me as fat.

I felt amazing, though scared—after spending three decades obese—to think I could spend the next three decades fit.

◇◇◇

I had been afraid of amusement parks ever since I started putting on weight, mostly because I was too fat to go on any rides. Now, eighty pounds down—the size of not such an obese person—I decided it was time to start doing things I'd never done before. Maybe even skating or a ropes course—but I wanted to start with a roller coaster because Anna had requested a visit to Universal Studios Orlando in lieu of a party.

As we boarded the plane, my instinct was to ask a flight attendant for a seatbelt extender. It was what I had always done, subtly, quietly but loudly enough for the overworked flight attendant to hear me over passengers loading luggage into overhead compartments.

When I settled Emily and Anna into their spots, making sure each one had their own set of headphones and had the televisions tuned to what they wanted to see, I was about to go ask for one.

But as I saw the gray seatbelt hanging from the seat, I thought maybe I should just try it. Making sure the girls' eyes were fixed forward on their screens, I pulled it over my lap as far as it would go, again making sure other passengers weren't looking as I found the other end dangling in the aisle. I took a deep breath in, and then forced my hands together until I heard a "click."

Oh. My. God. It fit.

It pressed into the fat on my hips, tight and a bit uncomfortable, but it fit. The two pieces connected, which was something that hadn't happened in years. I wanted to stand up and celebrate, but of course I couldn't because I was now belted in. I looked up to see Chris's eyes fixated on the buckle. He smiled and nodded. I smiled, too.

If airplane seatbelts fit, I wondered what awaited me at Universal Orlando. Anna couldn't wait to experience the Wizarding World of Harry Potter. And now, neither could I.

As I stood in line for the Flight of the Hippogriff with my daughters and Chris (Elliott stayed home with my in-laws), my hands were shaking, even though there were toddlers in line with us. Both Anna and Emily were bouncing with anticipation. I could hear people shrieking with excitement, fear, and all those things I hadn't let myself feel.

But I especially didn't feel them on a roller coaster.

As the roller coaster car crawled up the hill and then around the first bend, I wanted to hold on, to brace myself for the next turn. But somewhere, while I was screaming my head off, I decided to let go and just enjoy the ride.

Once I did that, it was the ride of my life. And it opened the door for all sorts of other rides. Instead of sitting things out, I happily went along, screamed myself hoarse, and wondered what the next thrill would be.

Isn't that what life is? Building up to places you don't want to go, only to get through them, screaming, sweating, afraid everything is going to topple and fail. It is only when you are willing to go for the ride that you're able to enjoy it.

After the ride (thankfully not before), we stopped at the Three Broomsticks Café. Chris and I shared a breakfast plate. I was now used to ordering smaller portions, such as an appetizer, or just sharing an entrée. If I ordered a burger or chicken sandwich, I used the bread to hold it as I ate the meat inside. At this breakfast, we all enjoyed eggs and sausages. I skipped the croissants.

"Well, at least I'm saving us money," I said, taking a forkful of eggs. I had gotten used to prioritizing protein on my plate. Chris smiled.

I looked at him lovingly. I loved the way his eyes sparkled when he laughed. It was as if I hadn't seen that in a while. It was probably always there, but I hadn't noticed.

There was such beauty in that moment, of feeling alive. The girls made their way through their eggs, in the bustle of the restaurant, as if there was magic far beyond anything Harry Potter had to offer, and it was that very moment.

I was still afraid of numbers. The ones with dollar signs. The ones on the scale.

So, on the day my husband and I were finishing our taxes and Anna proposed making cookies, I faced a double threat.

So I faced a dilemma—do I make cookies with her or was that feeding my tax-induced stress?

One of the tricky things about the surgery was that I really could eat just about anything, just not as much. It made me sometimes wish I had had the gastric bypass so I'd have to be stricter about my food intake.

I stood at the kitchen counter, pressing my palms against the cold granite. I did this when I was stressed, taking a moment to feel grounded, connected to something. I allowed the cold to seep into my cells. This was a new thing, something I did as I taught myself to slow down instead of just reaching into a box of cereal for comfort. I took a few breaths and thought through my response.

Anna had been binge watching those kids baking championship shows. Shows like them presented a bit of a paradox. They were well produced, with drama, creativity, and the fantasy of creating world-class confections.

But a whole enterprise was built on them. I mean, people at the gym watched the Food Channel when they worked out. Sometimes I watched the Food Channel when I worked out. Sometimes I wouldn't have it on the treadmill screen, but I had lovingly stared at the screen, ignoring myself, sweating through the recipe.

Seriously, spending time with Pioneer Woman Ree Drummond as she cooked a picnic suitable for hungry cowboys could get me through any incline on the treadmill. It seemed like she had a healthy relationship with food. She was big, but not too big. She was an award-winning blogger, best-selling author, and worked on a ranch in Oklahoma. She had it all.

Why couldn't I enjoy food and cooking like she did?

With my own daughter, would telling her she couldn't make the cookies be restricting her creativity or her appetite? Thereby swinging her too far to the other side of the pendulum? Her weight was fine. What was I afraid of?

I didn't want her to bake cookies because I didn't want to be tempted to eat them.

But should I allow her to make the cookies in support of her culinary ambitions? Should I not allow her to make the cookies because they wouldn't ease the uncertainty of our tax bill?

When I walked the line of a normalized pattern of eating, eating like everyone else, there was so much to consider. This was the work of recovering from Binge Eating Disorder. Work I had to do even after the surgery.

For one, what was a healthy way of thinking about food? For some people, it was about restricting something—no carbs, only raw, gluten free, Paleo. For me, it was about making sure I felt nourished with good foods, not processed foods.

Something else to consider was my history of food behaviors. When I was a kid, I had my own sweet dreams. I had ordered candy cookbooks from mail-order book clubs. I even got a candy thermometer. I boiled sugar and made taffy, stretching and pulling it to the perfect consistency. I often did this by myself, mostly so I could binge on the results.

And though I might have shared some with my family, most was gone by the time they returned home.

One day, when Anna came home from the book fair with a copy of the Food Network's *Sweet: Our Best Cupcakes, Cookies, Candy, and More* cookbook, I didn't know what to think.

"Wow," I said, terrified that she was opening the same doors I had at that age. But she put it away and quickly forgot that she bought it.

Learning about Binge Eating Disorder and the neurobiology behind it made me aware that I was prone to food cues. Marketing, a flashy TV spot blasting in the other room, could set my brain on fire with wondering how to get a bite of the gooey, new creation that was being advertised. And each time I thought of food, I had to remember it was my brain that was going into overdrive. I was the one who had to slow it down.

I had stomach surgery, not brain surgery. I had to work with the brain I had.

But cooking also took the immediacy out of eating, forcing me to wait instead of reaching for the nearest junk food, which was a lot less prevalent in our house since the surgery. There was the pause to gather ingredients from the store, from the cupboards. To measure and mix. To truly become a craftsman. Baking, especially, wasn't about haste but about methodical and deliberate amounts of ingredients, all mixed together.

The process of cooking and baking helped me appreciate what food was made of and how I could enjoy it more. I hoped that if I did this with my daughter Anna, we would learn *together*. We would take the time to craft a dish, make it our own, instead of scarfing down a whole package of something and barely noticing that it was gone.

I pulled down the flour from the cabinet, sending a puff of white powder across the counter top. I preheated the oven to 350 degrees.

Anna opened the fridge to get the butter, sending a cold whoosh over my shoulder. And so we began.

She held the mixer and I held the bowl, and we beat sugar, eggs, and butter. In a matter of moments, they whipped together, ready for the flour. She dipped her finger in the bowl to take a taste and so did I.

"Mmm," she said. "Perfect."

"Indeed," I said.

The cookie sheets clanged as I pulled one out for our concoction. Anna spooned the mixture onto the sheet.

"That's big enough," I said.

"Like this?" she asked, plopping down about two teaspoons full, half as much as she had planned on before.

"Perfect," I said.

This was the elusive middle ground I was looking for. To find the joy in food, not the emotional delay. It wasn't covering anything up, it was just food, and there was joy in making it together. To see my daughter's accomplishment and skills blossoming.

We didn't do this every day, though she would have wanted to make cookies every day.

As a parent, it was my job to regulate, to be the guardrails, as she bumped through her relationship with food. We decided to create a "Make Something Wednesday" that would give her a day to look forward to cooking. She would plan the ingredients and then we'd make the item together.

The point was to include an element of pause and intention in what we ate, which was something I learned on my own journey, whether from CBT—Cognitive Behavioral Therapy—or ACT—Acceptance and Commitment Therapy—or one of the many other acronyms I encountered in my treatment and healing. It was the recipe to ensure that Anna had treats but that we weren't going off the deep end.

This was about building a relationship with Anna. This was about rebuilding a relationship with food around our values, what mattered to us.

That night, fresh peas from our garden were part of our dinner. Anna had picked the biggest ones from the towering trellis in our plot. She ate a few there and brought the rest home with pride.

I slammed the minivan door shut.

This time, there were no children to unload. Chris and I had driven down the New Jersey Parkway to the PNC Arts Center in Holmdel for a Bryan Adams concert. I saw the $20 tickets on Groupon and couldn't resist buying them, especially because we were trying to get out more together.

Also, I still kind of had a crush on my fellow Canadian, Bryan Adams. Of course I did. He was there for me as a kid.

"Wow, Bryan Adams still has a following," I said, as we parked the car in the general parking lot, which was quickly filling up. We skipped the VIP parking, even though it was right next to where the performance was, and opted for a walk. Mostly because it was more expensive.

The skies softened into evening on the half-mile walk to the venue, an open-air arena. The forest next to the path darkened but was highlighted by streetlights. My feet felt cool and damp in flip-flops. It was supposed to rain that night, but we didn't care. My rain jacket, which was tied around my waist, flapped as I walked. Our speed created a breeze, cooling off the humidity that stuck to my face that New Jersey summer evening.

The path turned a bit uphill, and Chris and I passed another couple who were going slower. As we passed each street lamp, I noticed my engagement ring sparkle. The little dazzling glow was back on my left ring finger and I would never take off again.

We found our spot on the lawn, sort of in the middle, angling for the best view. For once I wasn't worried about how others saw me. I wasn't hiding in the back. The ground was moist from a rain shower that had passed through earlier in the day, so I put my jacket down as a tarp. We weren't such regular concertgoers, so we hadn't thought to bring lawn chairs. I happily sat on the ground without worrying about how I'd get back up again.

I had been doing yoga for a couple months, and going from a seated position to standing was old hat now, something I did with ease and strength, even while among a crowd.

There was a little flutter in my heart, not just for Chris but for Bryan Adams. I could never afford to see him in the eighties, but now I was about to see him perform, in the flesh.

When he came on stage, I jumped up and screamed like a teenage girl. Chris sat and watched, smiling. I knew almost every word of his old songs. His raspy, gorgeous voice was the same as it was then. I had played his *Reckless* cassette again and again in my bedroom until the tape wore thin.

That was the same room where I hid food wrappers from binges. Where I buried my dreams, as I swooned and swayed to his music, clutching my pillow. Back then, I wanted someone to notice me, to care, to feed me with love. In that room, my father's photo sat on my hutch before I smashed it to pieces, angry that he had gone out of my life. In that room, Bryan Adams was my imaginary boyfriend.

One song above all others held me and comforted me: "Heaven." Six songs into the set, he played it.

When the first few bars of piano followed by the guitar's cry played, my whole body responded. My heart opened, my knees buckled. Tears just poured from my eyes. I looked up and saw the clouds open to stars.

The words enveloped me. Especially, *"Once in your life you find someone. Who will turn your world around. . . . Bring you up when you're feeling down."*

In that moment, I could feel, truly feel the emptiness and sorrow of those days, those moments of pain—the feeling of my body being violated, the agony of waiting for my father only to be disappointed, the need for attention from my mom—they resurfaced all at once. I could feel it and, for a moment, it was too painful to bear. It was too much all at once.

Chris wrapped his arms around me. We kissed and I dug my head into the curve of his neck, feeling his warmth and support. I turned back to watch Bryan Adams play, the lights blurry in my watery eyes. To hear the entire audience sing in unison was to have the words wrap around me and fill that hole in my heart with love. This love was truly mine. For one moment, I could accept that, not fear it was going away.

It didn't hurt that Bryan Adams was right there singing it.

This was a song of my past, but it was playing in my present. "Heaven" was one of our wedding songs, but I don't think I truly realized how much it represented us and how much love I had, because I had pushed it away for so long.

"Are you okay?" Chris asked.

"I've never been better," I said, holding his hand. His fingers wrapped around my wedding band. We kissed again.

When I listened to the song in the eighties, I was so alone. Desperate to have that feeling of connection, anything. I found it in food. But now I had something else, something far more effective. With each day that I didn't turn to food, I realized how much I had to be grateful for, as if I had been awakened to the beauty. That's what I had all along with Chris, but now I was starting to realize the beauty of it.

"Just hold me now 'cause our love will light the way."

There are no easy ways out in life, and that is okay. If I got through the hard parts, I could arrive at this place of love and wonder.

"Love is all that I need and I found it there in your heart. It isn't too hard to see we're in Heaven . . ."

Heaven.

The sun kissed each ripple of water flowing through Eldorado Canyon. The air was a bit thinner and so was I. I got out of the car about forty-five minutes west of Denver. With my weight about eighty pounds down after the surgery, I didn't feel any altitude sickness. However, the dry air made my throat and tongue feel like a wrung-out sponge, so I pulled on my water bottle and tied my turquoise fleece jacket around my waist. There was enough slack so that I could make a double knot at my belly button.

I was hiking for fun but also for work. I had wanted to find a job that would support healing my body and mind, and I found one. I became a National Recovery Advocate for Eating Recovery Center and shared my story to help others who struggled with Binge Eating Disorder. Each time I told my story, the more the shame and guilt of my own complicated relationship with food fell away.

Instead of my weight being my life, my recovery was now what I lived and breathed. It felt good and real. I loved bringing a voice to a struggle that until a few years ago didn't have a name in the *Diagnostic and Statistical Manual,* a book health professionals use to determine a patient's diagnosis.

I was in Colorado to tell my story of recovery in a podcast called *Mental Note.* The producers, Ellie and Sam, wanted to get me talking on a trail, a place that felt natural to me.

It was just a morning jaunt—two hours before heading back to get cleaned up for a meeting and then my speaking event in downtown Denver. But it felt good, finally, to talk about my journey. My way of being and the weight of being without using food.

On that hike, I never felt so free. At 265 pounds, I had been physically lighter in my adult life, but to me, I felt strong in my feet as I pushed up the mountain and continued to take positive steps in my wellness.

The previous week, I had kissed Anna's blonde head and left her with a counselor and tent mates at a Vermont sleepaway camp. The girls immediately went to the tetherball pole and started to play. She was active, free, and strong, and she had recently fallen in love with basketball and run a 5K. I knew three and a half weeks in the fresh air of Vermont would be good for her, a break from screen time, to explore her passions. She could take in all the beauty of the Green Mountains without the complications of my childhood. I was so happy to be able give this to her. She immediately wrote (as she did every day on Emoji stationery) that she was having so much fun and had fallen in love with archery.

We were both on target.

I was truly happy. Many pounds lighter with still a lot to lose but having gained so much.

My goal with the weight loss surgery was not to transform my body but to take off enough pounds so I could be the person I strived to be. Someone who could participate fully in life. I wasn't putting off my to-do list because it seemed to be too treacherous or overwhelming. Like this hike: step by step I could make it to the top. And bit by bit, I could take on the little things of daily life without food getting in the way.

And when I compared my body—eighty pounds heavier the previous summer, when all I felt was pain and struggled even to move—this hike, these activities were amazing. I wasn't dragging around all that extra mass any more.

I had to go to the bathroom but held it for the composting toilet near the gate. I realized that it was the first time in a while that my hiking pants didn't reek of urine after my body couldn't wait to go. Even my bladder seemed stronger and under less pressure after some weight loss. That was a relief.

Even though my body had changed, nothing about me was that different. But the ways I handled life were.

I was still an anxiety-ridden mother. I worried about Anna going to camp but knew that she was going to have an amazing adventure. If something was gnawing at me, I reached out to Chris, Marnie, or a friend.

In the past, I procrastinated when the school forms came home and would wait until I got a reminder email that my child wouldn't be able to start a program without the paperwork. Now I found pleasure and relief in getting things done—from filling school forms to paying medical bills. I mapped out my day, including my meals, and didn't fall into the trap of grazing all day long. I knew what was coming, so when something unexpected happened, it was easier to deal with.

But I also allowed for flexibility.

I exhaled the thoughts about doom and disaster. When I beat myself up about money, I got to work to find some more. The more I was true to myself, the more I found opportunities to tell my story. If I had a project to finish, I started it instead of allowing myself to be swallowed by food or Facebook. I was dealing with life. Not always in the best way, but I was doing the best I could with what I had.

Just before dropping Anna off, we'd stayed at my mother's house, but my mom didn't focus on the kids much. She worried about making meals instead of playing with them; she didn't engage more than by brushing the girls' hair. She was worried about the kids breaking the antiques or falling into the well. After four days of tension, one morning the two of us had a pow-wow before the kids awoke.

"I see Anna and she reminds me of you when your dad and I got divorced. That's when I stopped really knowing you. I felt really sad about that," she said, looking down at her coffee. That's when my mother had to focus on making a living and a life apart from my father.

"Mom, we can't change the past. But you can know Anna now. She's right here," I said.

That day, she spent time with Anna helping her orchestrate a lemonade stand, something my serial entrepreneur daughter loved to do.

"I worry about her being so close to the road," my mother said.

"I do too," I said. But we both knew she would be fine as she hung out with Emily and her fifteen-year-old cousin Hannah by the road.

That night, Chris took me out to a beer festival. Microbrews were one of my favorite things on the planet. Even though they were difficult to drink because of the carbonation, I wasn't quite willing to give them up in the same way that I had sworn off Perrier, soda, and other fizzy things. Still, I drank in moderation. And because the Vermont Brew Fest was all about trying beers, I could take a sip and dump the rest on the grass.

My friend Megan from high school met us there. Along the Lake Champlain shore, we went from tent to tent laughing. Megan used to call me "One-Can Kara" because of my low tolerance in high school. Now, my tolerance was even lower.

I only sipped from the little tasting glasses, except for the one with Lawson's Liquids Maple Nipple. That one was delicious and down the hatch, followed by a large, satisfying belch that went unnoticed by the jovial beer crowd.

I still loved beer, especially the fruity and weird ones. I appreciated the craftsmanship of each one. This wasn't about polishing off a pint; it was about enjoying the flavor.

"Are you feeling any aftereffects from the surgery?" Megan asked.

"Not really," I said. "Maybe it was too easy. I can eat almost anything. Even ice cream."

"Slips right through, eh?" Megan said with a laugh.

"So, even though I had the surgery, I know I'll have to be careful the rest of my life."

"We all do," she said.

This should have comforted me, to know that I was just like everyone else now. But it terrified me. I worried about how I would use food for my life. How would I inter-pret it going forward? Because food was a relationship I had to have, I needed to keep learning and processing.

Some things did come more naturally to me after the surgery: for example, feeling full. Not going for seconds. Eating healthful and nutritious foods first (well, most of the time).

Surgery wasn't the easy way out. It was a tool to treat the symptoms of obesity. In other words, the resulting quick weight loss immediately helped my knee, which felt new again.

Binge Eating Disorder is squarely based in neurobiol-ogy. Thus, my work to recover from this disorder was to "rewire" my brain. In life, where we must have food to sur-vive and can't avoid it entirely, I had to learn how to adapt differently to the brain I had. I still faced the same urges and vulnerabilities, such as when I was sleep deprived. I knew that meant taking better care of myself—getting enough sleep and asking for what I needed.

The morning after the beer fest, I woke up on the air mattress at my mom's with a bit of a headache, even though I had had the equivalent of a beer and a half over three hours. Chris and the kids were sleeping all around the room we shared while we were there.

The air mattress creaked as I hoisted myself up and out of bed and headed downstairs in search of Tylenol and water. (Since the surgery, ibuprofen was kind of a no-no, to protect the lining of my stomach.)

It would be our last day all together as a family before Anna left for camp. I poured myself a cup of coffee, pressed my hands into the warmth of it, and took some bariatric vitamins.

Thinking about Anna out of our house for nearly a month while she was at camp cast a wave of sadness over me. I held my coffee tighter, letting the steam caress my cheek. In this moment of mindful pause, I decided: *Today, we hike.*

I went into the downstairs bathroom, an expansive room with a hot tub and shower in the corner, to find my suitcase. I flopped open the lid and pulled out the pants I had worn on my first Kilimanjaro hike, when I was 240 pounds. Perhaps it was too soon, because I was hovering around 260 on a bit of a plateau nine months after the surgery. But I wanted to try them anyway. They looked like adventure pants, with pockets down the side and little loops to pull them up into capris.

My stomach fluttered. Last time I had tried on pants this size it was to a heartbreaking end on that second trip to Kilimanjaro. That failed climb, when I had to have two pairs of pants sewn into one and turned back down the mountain before reaching the summit, launched a set of disastrous consequences that included the worst binge of my life: I demolished a gallon-size bag of chocolate. These smaller pants, which weren't used to patch together a pair that would fit me then, had ended up stored in my attic. They were even too small for my third climb a few years later.

But clothes had started fitting again, and I was willing to try these. I looped them over my ankle and then over my hips.

They felt easy and natural. I buttoned them, with room to spare. They fit!

I did a little happy jig and turned around to see myself in the mirror over the vanity. Though my rear was still large and my hips were somewhat protruding, I looked—and felt—healthy again.

Healthy was a feeling. My body still had the same general shape, but the muscles were stronger, more able, and my movement was freer. And on this day, we were going to hike.

And it wasn't Chris's suggestion; it was mine.

This time felt different from the first time I dropped a lot of weight. Now I knew when to ask for support. I knew that if I fell, I needed to ask for help to get back up. There were plenty of people willing to extend a hand: my husband, my friends, my therapist (who I made a point to see at least every other week), my community on Facebook sites such as Binge Eating Connection and Bariatric Eating.

I poured cool filtered water into our water bottles and packed a diaper bag for the jaunt. It wasn't going to be a huge hike, just Mount Philo, but one that we could all— even Elliott—do as a family.

I went to get Elliott's stroller out of the trunk.

"No, don't worry, he doesn't need it," Chris said.

"Okay, but you're carrying him if he gets tired," I said, pulling the front door closed.

Emily marched ahead in her self-proclaimed "line-leader spot," and Anna went with her to keep an eye out.

With each step over the rocks, I didn't remember how easy this hike was. Maybe that's because it never was— everything before was a struggle. Chris helped me carry Elliott, with flailing limbs, over a steeper section of rocks. Everything.

It wasn't an easy hike, but it was easier.

In the past, by that point, I would have said we had to turn back, for whatever reason but truthfully because I was overwhelmed by the challenge. But here we were, all heading up the mountain in the same direction, at the same pace.

We were in it together.

Afterward, we went out for maple creemees (Vermont-speak for soft serve ice cream) as a family, but the real treat was the togetherness.

Beep. Beep.

"I'm going to have to check your thighs and groin area," the TSA agent blared out. She pointed to the monitor where yellow blocks appeared on the hips and thighs of the body scan image.

I had heard it before. Even with weight loss, this happened every time I was at the airport. The millimeter wave scan, the kind where you step on the yellow footprints and hold your hands up above your head, always thought I was hiding something in my hip area. No matter how wide a stance I took, there was still a mass of leftover fat in that area. While some people were checked for fabric—socks or jeans bunched around their ankles—I was given a lower-body pat-down each time I flew.

"Do you want a private screening?" she asked.

"No, just get it over with," I said, rolling my eyes. "What do you think you're going to detect that isn't just fat?"

"Aw, you're beautiful," she said, slipping her hands inside my waist band. She meant to be nice, but it felt icky. The security guard, with her hair tied in a tight bun and her eyeliner curling up on her eyelids, practically gave me a karate chop to the crotch.

Food might have saved me from emotions that were too complex to process as a child, but that set me up for a tortured relationship with it throughout my lifetime.

I was infuriated that I was the victim—and was being treated instead like a criminal.

The agent finished her pat-down and then swiped my hands to make sure I hadn't been handling explosives. Every time, they found nothing. Just fat.

So, had I made myself a criminal? Was this body I created, this extra weight, a symbol of my punishment? Was that my Sisyphus—my boulder?

Anna looked back nervously.

"Mom, what's wrong?" she asked, as I put my shoes and belt back on, red in the face from the experience.

"Their machine has a glitch in it. It thinks I'm hiding something," I said, winking at her. "But I've got nothing to hide."

And it was true. I was not hiding anymore. I was traveling the country, sharing my story, my challenges with my body, and my food. Each time I did so, I stripped away the layers of shame that held me back.

I didn't know how long it would be before my

saddlebags shrank, but these experiences made me think it might be worth getting rid of them surgically. Though I fit better in an airline seat, I still overrode my allotted space and pushed under the armrests of my neighbors. At my heaviest—and traveling with my kids—I'd lift the armrests just to have some relief. Once when I was traveling at well over the 320-pound mark, I made sure I booked a first-class seat and felt like a hot shot. My weight was costing me.

With a disorder fueled by shame and low self-esteem, being called out as different or defective was the ultimate insult. I had put myself in the place of vulnerability. Humiliation is a side effect of Binge Eating Disorder. Humiliation has clung to me ever since kids in school thought it was funny to target me for my weight. For decades, I had been the butt of other people's jokes about my butt.

I knew this extra checking was for security. I was a newspaper reporter during September 11; that day is still with me. I sat in the living rooms of families who hoped their husbands, wives, children would come home. I reported when body parts were found.

Of course I wanted the planes to be safe. I simply wished TSA could find a way to detect whether anomalies were organic or something else. But it was up to me to learn strategies so these experiences didn't ruin me.

As I learned to love myself where I was, and go from there, I took on new habits for me and my family. I thought about what other changes were down the road for me, how

I could take my body to the next level. Even though I had dropped a good eighty pounds, and my face and breasts were slimmer to the point that moms at school pickup took notice and told me how good I looked, I knew my success wasn't necessarily measured by pounds but by what I did with my stress.

In the case of being felt up in the airport, victory was me not binging away the skeevyness of the groping in the name of national security.

My body was the same as it was when I was younger— a pear. I was tiny on top, wide on the bottom. My yoga teacher once said that you hold anger in your hips. If that was the case, I still had a lot to let go.

I wondered if liposuction and a body lift would finally get rid of it. I know, I know. It wouldn't. That work I need to keep doing in my mind.

Still, perhaps, I could start the process of plastic surgery.

The part of me that didn't allow my girls to have Barbie dolls screamed that this was a terrible idea. But my weight was literally in the way, still, a year after surgery. Wasn't self-acceptance, not self-deprecation, to go one step further into my body?

I still haven't decided. And until I do, I'll be setting off alarms at airports.

I was having a rough week. Our new au pair, Tina, who had arrived from Poland three months prior, just quit to work for a family with less kids, and I worried that Anna, who adored her, was going to be heartbroken. Now I had no child care, and a big deadline loomed. Plus, I was still smarting from a root canal and an infection deep in my jawbone, the result of a lifetime of sugar eating away at my teeth. *Sigh.*

I knew I'd have problems as a thinner person. I knew I'd feel miserable sometimes. But, with binging off the table, I wasn't sure what to do to feel better.

Mostly, I worried about Anna. She didn't know Tina left yet—she was away at camp—so I had a few days to consider how I would tell her, and I was gut wrenched, imagining her reaction. She had helped pick Tina from hundreds of young women an ocean away, and she clicked with her. Sometimes, when they were giggling together, they seemed more like sisters than baby-sitter and charge. When Tina said she was leaving, it felt as though she were breaking up with us.

With Anna.

My reaction was strong, ugly, and hard.

I started to recognize this feeling, as it ached in the pit of my heart, as abandonment. The very same feeling I felt when my father left. I couldn't bear for Anna to experience that feeling. I didn't want her heart to shatter in the same way that mine had.

That night, sleepless, I found myself in the kitchen opening the cabinet. I pulled out a mug, heated some water, and added a tea bag to it. I sat down at the counter and felt the cool granite against my forearms. I put my hands around the cup and felt the warmth seeping in.

I exhaled. My shoulders felt heavy with the task ahead of telling Anna, and my body was absorbing my stress in a way that had gone unnoticed when I was binging.

I tried to reassure myself that Anna would be okay. Tina wasn't an official family member, and no one was dying. That realized, I remembered that my brain could sometimes overestimate responses. I lived in danger-response mode, seeking a crisis. The more I breathed and looked at the situation, the more I recognized that perhaps, although Tina was important, this wasn't going to be the end of the world.

Most things weren't. Still, it was okay for me to process and understand that overreaction, to go deeper in ways to keep me and my family healthy.

Later, when my friend Marybeth invited me for a hike, I said yes. The thing about hiking is that it gives you a long stretch of time to walk and talk. You can come back to the same conversation again and again over different terrain and have a completely different perspective.

I confessed to Marybeth that I was overreacting but that I also couldn't help it. I didn't want to see Anna's heart broken when there was nothing I could do. How would Anna cope?

That's when I realized why I was so worried for Anna. I was nine years old when my dad left and I turned to food to survive. It was the beginning of my tumultuous relationship with eating. This, it seemed, was a juncture in her life where things could take her down a bad path.

I had recently learned that 50 percent of children who have an obese parent will also struggle with obesity. I didn't want a loss to send Anna into that half of the kids who sought comfort with food. Not Anna! And not now, when we both had come so far.

Marybeth was helpful. She reminded me that to help Anna I had to help myself. I was doing all the right things, putting one foot in front of the other. I had to keep working through life. Keep doing the things that brought me joy. Keep working through the experiences that brought me sorrow, knowing that I didn't need food to help me recover from them.

Life with a healthy relationship with food wasn't perfect, she acknowledged. It was messy, ugly, and complicated. But problems like these could be managed.

As we turned a corner in the trail, sweaty from walking for more than a mile, Marybeth had one more important reminder: Anna was not being abandoned.

Abandonment and food issues were mine. They didn't have to be Anna's.

"There was no one for you when you were going through those things. All you had was food," she said. "She has you."

And so she does.

All my life, my eyes have been bigger than my stomach.

Until now.

Portion control was something I really needed to work on, even postsurgery, but I just couldn't get myself to place a helping of food into a measuring cup before dishing it out to myself. What a chore. It was silly, but it held my progress back for some time.

Like many people who have struggled with weight, I had portion distortion. It didn't matter how many times a nutritionist told me that a proper serving of meat or fish was about the size of the palm of my hand or a deck of cards. If I was going to get serious, and I knew measuring cups were a barrier to success, I had to think of another way.

One day as I was looking through my cabinets, I came upon a heart-shaped ramekin that had arrived free from Le

Creuset when I ordered something else as a gift. We only used it for special occasions or as a cereal bowl when one of the kids was feeling down. And, of course, on Valentine's Day.

Wasn't it about time that I gave myself the same love, with a heart-shaped bowl?

My body wasn't Barbie's. It was so much more.

But I could move with grace again. Do yoga. Even dance at a wedding. Most importantly, I hiked.

The only thing that had slowed down was my eating because of a physical barrier that prevented me from eating beyond a set amount. Feeling full was something that, like a lot of people with Binge Eating Disorder, was foreign to me before the surgery. If I tried to eat more, I felt uncomfortable, and that was a cue to stop.

I was sure my stomach had stretched beyond its original four-ounce pouch. Every now and then, I'd eat a yogurt and notice that it was 5.3 ounces. But here's the thing, I'd consume the yogurt over twenty minutes. I shuddered to think how much food I ate in twenty minutes before the surgery. A regular-sized stomach can hold two liters— think of a large soda bottle.

But now four ounces (give or take) was my limit.

Sometimes I worried that I'd stretch it out and fall into the pattern of eating what was served to me instead of taking only what I could manage or that I'd eat high-caloric things or go back to milkshakes. Some people who struggle with Binge Eating Disorder have done that.

My goal was to eat like most people do. And although I was not really a fan of lamb anymore (Caryn was right), I could eat most of the things I liked. Just less.

I figured that if I measured the ramekin once, I would know exactly how much it held and could use that as a guide to track my portions. I filled it with water and then emptied it into a measuring cup. It held about six ounces. I then measured four ounces and made a mental note as to where to stop filling the bowl.

In the cold weather, I loved to eat soups and chilis, so this was going to be my way of keeping track while having a lovely little lunch in a heart-shaped bowl. What a nice reminder that each meal was a celebration, an opportunity to do something loving for myself.

I adored this bowl so much that while I was traveling through Lake George on my way to speaking engagements and a visit to my mom in Vermont, I stopped at a Le Creuset outlet. There, I found a blue heart bowl and purchased it along with a pretty set of ramekins with lids. Each one was a lovely color. If I was making a casserole for my family, I could dish out a few portions to keep for lunch that week.

That I shopped at the Lake George outlets and did not eat was significant. Because I lived in New Jersey but grew up in Vermont, I traveled through that area often. In the past, it was my place to stop to refuel on snacks for the final two hours in the car before reaching South Burlington.

I loved when one little change—a heart-shaped bowl—could break other habits for the better.

Though there was less food, the rest of my life was fuller.

I was okay with that.

But there was this: I was really, really happy.

And when I was sad, I was really, really sad.

I don't numb myself out with food, preventing myself from feeling the sadness. But it wasn't like I didn't have a safety net or support; I had Marnie to help me with this.

As I headed to Marnie's office, I looked at the elevator and noticed that there was a staircase right next to it. I walked the flight up, something I would do from that point on.

I landed on her couch instead of in the chair.

"That's interesting," she said. "You're on the couch this week. Most patients pick a spot and always go to that spot."

The reason I moved from the chair to the couch was because I no longer needed the arms on the sides to help hoist myself up. But if that was a signal that I was more open to change, I was willing to go with that too.

We talked about frustrations, coordinating a new event, Tina's departure, how to bring up an expense with

Chris. We talked through solutions and created an action plan for each thing. These appointments were paramount for me and my healing as I forged a positive relationship with food.

Before, I would let problems swell and clog my mind and then block them with food. Now I was willing to work them out with another person. I was willing to admit that I needed help doing this, which saved me from pushing away everything with food. I was surrounded by more support, less fat.

I was in this body completely, ready for anything life threw at me.

Acknowledgments

There are so many people to be grateful for, but specifically for this book, I am so appreciative to the team who pushed me to dive deep into my experience and who helped make *The Weight of Being* a reality.

First, of course, is my family—Chris, Anna, Emily, and Elliott—for inspiring me to be healthier and share this world. My in-laws, Robin and Jim, showed me more love and support than I have ever known. I couldn't have done this project (and most of what I do, really) without them. Thanks also to our au pairs Pauline and Claire, who have helped me so I can share my story with the world and take care of myself along the way. My dear friends who guided me through this process. My mother and brother Derek provided almost daily support as I processed my past for the page.

Thank you to my agent, Kim Perel, and editor, Laura Mazer, for their belief in my work and craft and for pushing for my voice (and so many others') to be heard. You, along with the team at Seal Press and Hachette, and my friend and editor Paula Derrow made this book possible, and I'm so incredibly grateful.

I must acknowledge Dr. Ragui Sadek and the team at Advanced Surgical & Bariatrics and the supporting physicians, especially Dr. Devang Patel, who moved heaven and earth to make sure I was ready for surgery and for taking such good care of me.

And for help in the now, I am so thankful to Marnie Grossman, who keeps me laughing as I work through the hard stuff and who teaches me to deal with life with grace and gumption.

To Eating Recovery Center, especially Doug Weiss and Dr. Julie Friedman, for sharing my story with so many people, for caring so deeply for people with Binge Eating Disorder, for helping them build a foundation for a healthy relationship with food. If you or someone you love may be struggling with Binge Eating Disorder, call 877-207-2419 or visit www.eatingrecoverycenter.com/kara.

And especially to you, dear reader, for coming to this book with an open heart. Sending love, peace, and strength your way.

About the Author

Kara Richardson Whitely is the author of *Fat Woman on the Mountain* and *Gorge: My Journey up Kilimanjaro at 300 Pounds*. *Wild* author Cheryl Strayed said of *Gorge*, "Kara is fearlessly honest and powerfully intelligent. I was moved and inspired by every page of this beautiful book." The *New York Times* cheered *Gorge*, "This detailed account of [Kara Richardson Whitely's] travails will give confidence not only to hesitant would-be mountaineers but to those, like her, whose biggest hurdle is 'to learn to be O.K. with who I was.'"

Kara also writes for publications that have included *Self, Rachael Ray Every Day,* and *Runner's World.* She has been featured on *Oprah's Lifeclass* and *Good Morning America* and in *Redbook, American Hiker,* and *Weight Watchers* magazine as well as on countless online media outlets, including Daily Beast, CNN, People, and Good Housekeeping.

Kara was a blogger for Weight Watchers and currently serves as an ambassador for the American Hiking Association. She is a National Binge Eating Recovery Advocate for Eating Recovery Center.

Kara travels the world sharing her story to inspire and empower others. She has presented at national conferences and companies, including Google, Sanofi, and Pfizer, as well as at universities such as Dartmouth and Purdue.

Kara, her husband, and their three children live in Summit, New Jersey. You can follow her adventures or book her for your event at kararichardsonwhitely.com.